DATE DUE

OC 23 01			
NO 19 01			
AP 29 03			
MY 19 03			
OC 7 03			
OC 30 03			
OC 31 03			
NO 7 03			
NO 15 03			

DEMCO 38-296

BOUNTY HUNTERS, MARSHALS, AND SHERIFFS

BOUNTY HUNTERS, MARSHALS, AND SHERIFFS

Forward to the Past

JACQUELINE POPE

Westport, Connecticut
London

Library of Congress Cataloging-in-Publication Data

Pope, Jacqueline.
    Bounty hunters, marshals, and sheriffs : forward to the past /
Jacqueline Pope.
        p.   cm.
    Includes bibliographical references and index.
    ISBN 0–275–94629–0 (alk. paper)
    1. Private investigators—United States.   2. Fugitives from
justice—United States.   3. United States marshals.   4. Sheriffs—
United States.   I. Title.
HV8088.P66   1998
363.28'2'0973—dc21   98–14929

British Library Cataloguing in Publication Data is available.

Library of Congress Catalog Card Number: 98–14929
ISBN: 0–275–94629–0

First published in 1998

Praeger Publishers, 88 Post Road West, Westport, CT 06881
An imprint of Greenwood Publishing Group, Inc.

Printed in the United States of America

∞

The paper used in this book complies with the
Permanent Paper Standard issued by the National
Information Standards Organization (Z39.48–1984).

10 9 8 7 6 5 4 3 2 1

Copyright Acknowledgment

Grateful acknowledgment is given to *Sheriff Magazine* and the National Sheriffs' Association for permission to reprint Ted Sattler's "The High Sheriff in England Today: The
Invisible Man?" (May–June 1992).

This book is dedicated to my mother and siblings, especially Nzinga.

Forward ever, backward never

CONTENTS

TABLES

PREFACE

A significant number of people think bounty hunters, city marshals, and sheriffs are as extinct as stagecoaches. Others know these law enforcers exist, but believe their responsibilities are marginal or minimal—unless one lives in small towns, rural areas, or urban communities. Such views are not grounded in reality. Bounty hunters, city marshals, and sheriffs continue to operate in the twentieth century. Moreover, they have substantial, vital, and sometimes dangerous roles in the criminal justice system. Their professions vary and date, historically, hundreds of years.

The bounty hunters' image in the criminal justice system has alternated between unsavoriness and glamor, judging from books and films. In the seventeenth and eighteenth centuries, law officers and private citizens hunted criminals for a fee; they still do. As will be illustrated, reward collecting in the twentieth century is a thriving and lucrative profession among private business people.

Today there is the dues-based National Association of Bail Enforcement Agents (bounty hunters), which offers, for a fee, national certification seminars for bail enforcement agents. I will provide more information on this organization and its founder in the first chapter. The profession of bounty hunting is probably as old as the first female profession or, as some would argue, goes back to Judas. Very little has changed since biblical times for bounty hunters; patience continues as the dominant feature in hunting, capturing, and returning fugitives to the courts.

Present-day and historical information on bounty hunters is sparse and diverse. To my knowledge, other than a few articles and reports, bounty hunters' and New York City marshals' and sheriffs' activities are virtually undocumented. Currently there are two bounty hunter authors, two movies (*Midnight Run* and *Bounty Hunter*), and a television program by the latter name. Consequently, true stories and interviews occupy a vital place in this research. It should be noted that two distinct interview methods were employed. This was unintentional; some people were more outgoing when responding to questions, while others preferred doing all the talking.

Occasionally bounty hunters make horrible mistakes during capture that generate headlines and discussions about the profession. However, once the spotlight dims, bounty hunters return to their obscure status and continue to be ignored by the media and public. Basically, federal, state, and local governments, even private citizens, employ bounty hunters to secure an individual's return to a designated location, usually within a specific time frame. Offering bounty is an age-old practice in the United States.

In the case of sheriffs, they are mentioned in the Bible's Old Testament, Book of Daniel. The profession, established in England under common law, was a thousand years old in 1992. City and town marshals, too, are patterned after an English institution, but are younger than sheriffs by hundreds of years. Town marshals and town and county sheriffs have at different times performed interchangeable duties, including functioning as bounty hunters. These lawmen have famous and glorious pasts. Some are infamous and recorded in history as legends. Indeed, they are the first national police force, dating back to 1789. In the 1990s, most marshals serve at the federal level.

This book details the twentieth-century and historical roles of bounty hunters, city marshals, and sheriffs together with city and county sheriffs. The relationship and cooperation among other law officers and local police will be examined. Those forgone issues and professions are so intertwined that researching one profession necessitated compiling information on all four. Twentieth-century writings about marshals and especially sheriffs tended toward biographies. History tells us western town marshals' and sheriffs' titles were interchangeable. Some of these lawmen also held positions simultaneously at any given time. Compounding this confusion, a few graduated to federal marshaldom, thereby necessitating a discussion of U.S. marshals on which there is much documentation. Hence, for clarity's sake a section is devoted to the latter because of the existence of city marshals.

Additionally, you will note the bailbonds system, in conjunction with bailbondspersons, require nearly a full chapter. Again, connectedness and interchangeability of the crime-stoppers' titles and professions are the reasons for that inclusion. Researching this work was akin to walking at night through an extremely elaborate maze covered with cobwebs.

The historical sections furnished throughout the text are self-explanatory in that they provide readers with the background, fundamental knowledge, and insight for this research. To place these sections in a colloquial context, we must know where we came from to know where we are going. In particular, bounty hunters' history, the subject of a television documentary, is quite exciting and equally so for frontier or 1800's sheriffs and marshals, the latter having been grist for countless movies. Also a comparison between these nineteenth- and twentieth-century law officers offers a complete picture, thus enhancing and enabling the public's discussions on the issues to be more informed.

This book's intrinsic purpose is to provide information and documentation about a little known sector of law enforcement and increase their visibility in conjunction with raising questions in the public arena about their authority. My research began with the intention of documenting just bounty hunters and city marshals in 1990, but as noted previously, the interlocking aspects were too complex to ignore. Four summers were spent in major libraries in the designated states while the remaining time encompassed interviews in Arizona, New Jersey, New Mexico, and New York. Obtaining interviews proved as difficult as researching. Tracking down people who were important to the effort was time consuming. Individuals were extremely reluctant to speak out, with most requests denied. Their stance conveyed the impression that public scrutiny is unwelcome. This is understandable since few professions embrace public disclosures and monitoring.

Nevertheless, such are the costs of conducting business in a democratic society. Moreover, it is incumbent upon residents to carry out their civic responsibilities: namely to demand and conduct a serious review of those men and women having the legal wherewithal to deprive people of their liberty (and sometimes life), especially when private entrepreneurial interests are involved. Maintaining an effective democracy is hard work, but satisfying in the long run. Among the questions addressed, along with recommendations, include:

- Are these law enforcers archaic?
- Do city marshals, sheriffs, and bounty hunters have too much, unaccountable authority?
- Should taxpayers allow private business' employees to assume the state's role of law enforcer, as in the case of bounty hunters?

- Can the responsibilities of bounty hunters and marshals be performed less expensively and more efficiently by state or city agencies?

- Are there any structural economic issues that need to be scrutinized?

- Is this an instance of the privatization of law enforcement at its worse?

Divided into three main parts dealing, respectively, with bounty hunters, city marshals, and city and county sheriffs, the text furnishes current and historical information about these law enforcement professions. The contemporary legal aspects, responsibilities, and contributions are documented, and a historical perspective from the 1800s and early 1900s is provided. Interesting true stories of encounters with these law enforcers are presented, as is material from interviews with bounty hunters, bailbondspersons, city marshals, and sheriffs. The book's final section offers a summary and recommendations about these crime fighters for the twenty-first century.

Given the subject's enormity, this book focuses on just four states— Arizona, New Jersey, New Mexico, and New York—but all these law enforcers operate in every state. City marshals and city sheriffs are exceptions. Similarities and differences among the four states are examined, excluding the regulations and roles of federal marshals, who operate under uniform standards. Essentially, along with comparison purposes, there are two other reasons for focusing on Arizona and New Mexico, located in sections of the country, with reputations of lawlessness and violence. Further these states, prior to statehood, spawned law enforcement legends and bounty hunting activities. Bounty hunters, sheriffs, and city and town marshals comprise integral aspects of Arizona's and New Mexico's shared histories and present day culture. In those states, frontier legends and stories occupy a special folklore niche, which holds true in people's memory and psyche throughout the United States.

New Jersey's and New York's histories are less colorful, yet still exciting and replete with lawmen who have titles the same as their frontier counterparts. However, their responsibilities differ in significant areas; arguably economic and social class, as well as their longevity in law enforcement annals, separate western and eastern crime fighters. Moreover, they functioned in an established political structure as well as other entrenched institutions. Hence, the northeast's comparison with the frontier's law enforcement of the same name is vital to understanding the entire picture.

Illuminated in subsequent chapters are pronounced differences and general similarities among the legal privateers and lawmen. Intentions are to increase the fundamental knowledge base about these officers together with enhancing general insight on this subject. Admittedly, in the 1990s, sheriffs are known and respected in many outlying areas across the United States. The chapter on and interviews with sheriffs acknowledge their continuing law enforcement importance. As during frontier days, they are still the only crime-stoppers for miles.

The survival of bounty hunters, city marshals, and sheriffs is curious in an era when massive public police departments are the norm in twentieth- and twenty-first–century life. Certainly, this issue requires documentation. The surrogate lawperson's continued participation along with sheriffs and expanding civil police forces are telling, and could be seen as chilling aspects about perceived law enforcement needs across the United States. Clearly illustrated is continuing acceptance of this phenomenon. Increasing and expanding laws, inherent with the requisite strategies to enforce adherence, demand national introspection before the twenty-first century arrives.

This book seeks to expand public awareness about lesser known law personnel, examine them, and explain the linkages. To a large extent these activities are undocumented and should raise many questions. Furthermore, I have provided a modicum of analysis centered on the perspective of people whose lives are impacted most often by bounty hunters and unknown crime-fighters. It is hoped that this book will generate public discussion and intensify research in the areas of criminal justice and human rights.

ACKNOWLEDGMENTS

Many people gave freely of their time, ideas, and encouragement. Their numbers are to long to list individually. Thus, I shall name a representative few. Harry (not his name), a bounty hunter, opened the doors for me to New York City marshals and other bounty hunters. Further, Harry, a poet and a humane and thoughtful person, showed me a bounty hunter's gentle side. Also Bob Burton and Stan Rifkin, the last of the "real" bounty hunters, were extremely helpful. Burton welcomed me into his home and shared numerous stories. Rifkin spent hours talking with me on the telephone, remembering the old days, even his childhood in the orphanage. To hear Burton and Rifkin tell it, bounty hunting actually seemed like fun. Is that what I want to do when I grow up?

Sheriffs Froehlich and Plousis in New Jersey, Russi and Capwell in New York, Bowdich in New Mexico, and Captain Klein in Arizona were fountains of information and anecdotes. You will read their comments throughout the text. I thank them for taking time from their busy schedules to meet with me.

Three New York City marshals agreed to be interviewed. Again, I received a gold mine of data and information; many thanks to all of them. Equally important were the two bailbondswomen from New Mexico and New York, who gave generously of their time. Readers will be fascinated by their stories.

My husband, Jeff Hochman, worked with me at every juncture and was a constant source of support. I am deeply grateful to him. I owe much to my typist and important friend, Sandra Moore, for her patience and calm in the face of numerous drafts. My "babies" are wonderful people and a well of inspiration. They keep me moving ahead.

Timely and sensible comments were contributed by former student Frank Carbonetti, as well as other workshop participants at the Twenty-fifth Conference of Minority Public Administrators: Theresa Cummings, Caroline Gray, Gwen Kelly, Sandra Young, and Doris Starkes. The fantastic staff in the Center for Southwest Research at the University of New Mexico, especially Nancy Brown (the best citation detective in the nation), have my sincere gratitude. In addition, the staff at the Arizona Historical Society Tucson were extremely helpful. Editing by my sister Jan put me back on track. Her work was much valued, along with Kathy Dutton whose efforts and awesome efficiency brought all of this together.

Finally, The Richard Stockton College of New Jersey provided a crucial sabbatical and full grant support. Without this outstanding institution I doubt the book would be published. My sincere appreciation is offered.

ABBREVIATIONS AND TERMS

ABBREVIATIONS

BBP	Bailbondsperson
BEA	Bail Enforcement Agent
DEA	Drug Enforcement Administration
DOI	Department of Investigation
FIST	Fugitive Investigative Strike Team
FOA	For Other Authorities
NCIC	National Crime Information Center
NYSID	New York State Identification
OMB	Office of Management and Budget
USM	United States Marshals
VSA	Virginia Sheriffs Association

TERMS

Bailbondsperson	A private business person who posts bonds
Bail or Surety	A bond posted to the court

Collar	An arrest made by a bounty hunter
Constable	A law enforcement officer who has similar responsibilities as sheriff
New York City Marshal	Mayoral appointed private entrepreneur working with businesses on debt collection and the city on parking violations
New York City Sheriff	A New York City civil servant working with the New York City Parking Violations Bureau on outstanding traffic tickets
Skip	A person, released on bail, who fails to appear for a court appearance
Surrogate	A proxy or representative

BOUNTY HUNTERS

TWENTIETH-CENTURY BOUNTY HUNTERS

Bounty hunters come in all shapes and sizes and represent all ethnic and geographic backgrounds and genders. Regardless of the state in which they operate, they are primarily European American men from the lower economic rungs of society, even ex-offenders. As traveling men, they like the thrill of hunting and capturing Mother Nature's most intelligent species. Three have achieved fame: Bob Burton and Ralph "Papa" Thornson (now deceased) in the West, and Stan Rifkin in the East. Rifkin's and Thornson's careers have been the subjects of motion pictures. Rifkin was also the subject of a documentary made for television and a Steve McQueen movie.

Bob Burton, president of the National Association of Bail Enforcement Agents, which has a thousand members, was a consultant for Robert DeNiro's movie, *Midnight Run*. Further, Burton's former students were featured in the 1996 television documentary "Bounty Hunters." These "old timers" believe their work is more an art than a profession. They always get their man (or woman) with limited violence to themselves or the hunted. In addition, two female bounty hunters, in New Mexico and New Jersey, were interviewed for this book. The two interviewees consider themselves primarily bailbondspeople; however, if a client should jump bail, these women would assume the role of bounty hunter, tracking, capturing, and returning the "skip" to jail. The slang word "skip" refers to a person who disappears once he or she is let out of jail by virtue of having posted bail. To jump bail is the same as to skip or skipping.

Exceptions are made when a client travels to a neighboring state. At that juncture, the bailbondswoman usually hires a bounty hunter or bail enforcement agent. There are little, if any, differences between a bounty hunter and bail enforcement agent, except age and longevity. Older, experienced bounty hunters prefer the former title and are proud of it. Currently, younger men and women in the profession consider Bail Enforcement Agents (BEAs) the proper designation.

All the same, despite their unusual and exciting careers, these bailbondswomen lead normal lives. Both are married and neither husband is in the profession. The New Mexico woman has children and often takes them to her office or court so they can be knowledgeable about their mother's business. She has been a bailbondswoman for twenty years, having started when her father owned the firm she now owns. The firm is managed by relatives, siblings, and cousins—a real family affair. The New Jersey bailbondswoman owned and managed her business alone. She had more clients than she could handle.

People called her constantly for assistance. Inmates, using their one permitted call, contacted her as did their family and friends. She was available to bail someone out of jail anytime of the day or night. She believes the service had to be provided in order to give back or help the community. Starting out as a prison guard, this bailbondswoman decided that she could be an important advocate for low-income people as a bailbondswoman. Twenty-five years later, she was still in the business helping in every way possible. She sadly noted that downsizing, fewer well-paid jobs, and expanded police presence are the impetus for the current increased numbers of clients.

There is no end in sight, unless the economy makes a vigorous rebound for those living below the poverty line and the prison industry wanes. Currently retired from bailbonds business, she directs an after school community center in a donated building with local government funding and volunteers. There are additional comments on these interesting women in the interview section.

Former police and military officers, private investigators, body guards, process servers, and soldiers of fortune are among the ancillary professional men and women who double as bounty hunters. Where bounty hunters were virtually only European American males, in the 1990s people of color are making new in-roads in this once exclusive occupation. Although generally reluctant to enter the profession, European American women and people of color have been attracted by the substantial rewards. At one juncture, people of color were basically used solely as informants, "snitches" in bounty hunters language. Interestingly, a May 1978 article claims that police are mobilizing a secret witness army to fight crime. This information was discussed in the *National Crime Reporter*. The publication, new at the time, listed reward notices for unsolved crimes, hence the article's title, "Bounty Hunter's Delight."

Legal Standing of Bounty Hunters

In the twentieth century, bounty hunters are employees of bailbondsmen and -women; some call themselves bail enforcement agents or bail recovery agents. Bondspersons provide money for bail or bond to ensure that defendants return to court on a required date. If the date arrives without an appearance by the defendant, a bounty hunter is hired to find the wanted person. He or she has a finite number of days, depending on state law, to return the bail jumper to the authorities and collect a fee, usually a percentage of the bail. There is no money earned after the due date. Thus, bounty hunters are working against the clock, keeping their eyes on the prize, hoping there will be a hefty reward for their efforts.

For novices, each case may yield around $400.[1] Experienced and well-known bounty hunters receive the highest percentages and could average $2,500 per case. "One professional Bounty Hunter received $78,000 for an apprehension"[2] due in large measure to his extensive personal contacts among bailbondspersons and local police. As a result, bounty hunters are very knowledgeable about defendants who post high bail. Further, these men and women can and do negotiate a higher percentage of the reward.

Finding a person can be relatively easy, yet boring. That is, patterns of missing persons emerge, according to the book on the subject. Determine the pattern, identify hangouts, hobbies, family and friends, and the way is clear for the capture and reward. To bounty hunters, this is as normal a job as carpentry or teaching. Of course, the boring features come into play, watching the residence (in bounty hunter parlance, a "stake-out") of the defendant as well as those of her or his family and friends. In some cases, bounty hunters hire people to conduct surveillance or perform the really dangerous work. However, bounty hunters usually operate alone or with a partner, at times, in urban East Coast areas.

After locating the person, actual capture can be extremely dangerous for both defendant and bounty hunter. Surprise is the bounty hunter's primary tool. A detailed appraisal of the defendant's premises and outside area are critical. Extensive experience in evaluating the situation can save lives and ensure collection of the reward. Do bounty hunters need search or arrest warrants to enter a bail jumper's residence? The answer is a resounding no. Can bounty hunters legally take people across state lines? Yes, they can and do. Rules of law and conduct under which police function have no relevance for bounty hunters. Says Bob Burton, "We have more arrest authority as a Bounty Hunter than any police officer does, but only in the narrow niche of the bail bond fugitive . . . When that person takes out a bail bond, they waive their rights."[3]

Bounty hunting requires networking, that is, locally, nationally, perhaps internationally developing and maintaining contacts, in conjunction with police desk sergeants or warrant officers, fugitive squads, and informers. The aforementioned people are vital aspects of the bounty hunter trade. Without law enforcement contacts, consent, and assistance, the bounty hunter is essentially prevented from earning a living in his or her field. Stated another way, bounty hunters are private entrepreneurial appendages of public law enforcement, operating on the latter's good will and acquiescence. As a result, bounty hunters strive conscientiously and diligently for local law enforcement approval and respect. Small or big, virtually no favor or task is denied a lawwoman or -man by bounty hunters. It should be noted that other self-employed professionals operate in a similar fashion. Forging contacts and ties, providing important clients with special services, these are employment survival strategies used in every profession in the twentieth century.

True Stories

A developer sold worthless Florida land throughout the United States. Charged with fraud, the man posted bail and returned home to Canada. Bounty hunters tracked him and subsequently brought him back to Florida against his will and with threats on the life of his young son. Fearing for the youngster's life, he said nothing, even when freedom was possible, at the border checkpoint. Handcuffed throughout the harrowing trip back to the United States, the man claimed he was physically abused. The bounty hunters' actions created a major incident between the United States and Canada.

In Canada's eyes, bounty hunters kidnapped a Canadian citizen; bounty hunters believed they were simply doing their jobs, to the tune of $10,000 or more. To the U.S. government it was an embarrassing but necessary procedure. Was extradition an issue? No. These two nations have extradition treaties. In fact, federal marshals are authorized to travel worldwide to return defendants, as will be detailed in a later section. Kidnapping was the major concern of both countries because bounty hunters from Canada and other nations may spirit U.S. citizens out of the country.

Recognizing, for all intents and purposes, a kidnapping problem, U.S. authorities charged and jailed the bounty hunters.[4] Nevertheless, it is likely they returned to their profession after completing their sentences. Remember, bounty hunting does not require formal qualifications or licenses unless, regarding the latter, they are private investigators. The aforementioned case is well known, having created an international incident. Similar processes occur on the local level every day without any notice from the public at large. Indeed, Mary Q. Public would likely approve of bounty hunters' tactics given the current climate of fear about personal safety and criminals. More information about bounty hunters' legal standing is detailed in the section on bail bonds companies. Next, an additional true story that concerns a woman and her contact with bounty hunters in the United States.

She stood at the stove flipping pancakes on the griddle, hair uncombed, her robe tied in a loose knot around her small waist. She had gained considerable weight during pregnancy. However, the weight quickly evaporated due to the subsequent divorce as well as caring for three sons: twins (one was severely retarded) and the eldest, a teenager. At ninety-eight pounds, less than five feet tall and with low blood pressure, she was tired all the time. The pancakes might help her gain weight, and the boys loved them. But most important, pancakes were filling. Annette (an alias) wondered why her teenage son was taking so long at the store. Did he stop to play basketball again? This time, she would definitely ground him for a month.

Hearing the bell ring followed by insistent knocking, Annette yelled to her four-year-old son not to open the door. Too late. Coming up the stairs were two European American men, each about six feet tall and hefty. Outraged, Annette demanded to know why they were in her home. Ignoring her question, one man ordered Annette to get dressed and come with him. If she refused, they would physically remove her, night clothes and all. Annette, frightened, did as she was told and got dressed. She asked for identification, but none was forthcoming. One man did remind her about jumping bail.

Annette had driven through a toll gate during a troubled weekend when she forgot to take her prescribed medicine for manic-depression. Annette begged them to wait for her teenage son, so as not to leave the twins alone. The bounty hunters refused her request and ushered her down the stairs into the car. She was taken back to New Jersey, having forfeited bail by failing to appear in court on the required date. The men, whom she later discovered were bounty hunters, bought her a sumptuous lunch along the way. Upon her return to jail, Annette remained incarcerated over a month until the hearing. At that time she was fined and released. A kindly neighbor cared for her children while she was imprisoned.[5]

It is unlikely the bounty hunters received a large fee in this case; nevertheless, every reward counts regardless of size. More important, experience is gained. As Bob Burton, author of *The Bounty Hunter*, admits, bounty hunting is an adventure. In a 1984 interview in the magazine *Law and Order*, he notes that the closer the bounty hunter comes to his target, the more intense and exciting are the adrenaline-related activities (130). One receives major highs; the thrill of victory—or the sting of defeat—come later. Notwithstanding the power, excitement, and independence, bounty hunters are bound by some laws regarding bail arrest. They must know and adhere to these laws at all times, and the laws differ from state to state. Thus, bounty hunters are wise to review the statutes prior to apprehension or the bounty hunters could find her-/himself under arrest. Hence, making contact with local law enforcers is critical. Otherwise the Bounty Hunter could find her-/himself in an untenable position during the capture process. This is especially true when a fugitive has roots in the community and is well liked. Sometimes neighbors might come to the fugitive's aid. Furthermore, law officers can be very territorial regarding apprehensions in their precinct and town, particularly when the bounty hunter disregards the required courtesy call to the station, advising police officers of two things: (1) the presence of a bounty hunter, and (2) a fugitive. Ignoring this unwritten law is foolhardy, and bounty hunters risk losing the reward.

Bounty hunters travel with the original bail documents and other papers describing and concerning the fugitive, including the fugitive's picture, height, weight, birthmarks, age, education, language, her or his background information regarding relatives, friends, hangouts, barbers, hairdressers, illnesses, needed medications, and addictions, together with FBI data. To apprehend the "skip," tried and true ploys are used for enticing the hunted and then catching them, usually with the help of lawmen or local people. In contrast to the earlier statement, would local people assist in the capture or inform on the wanted person? Yes, because the bail jumper may be disliked by his or her neighbors.

Ordinarily, money is the reason for cooperating, since bounty hunters may give people a few dollars for information. All in all, you may recall that police officers are the bounty hunters' best contacts. Since bounty hunters have no official identification, per se, other than a business card, Bob Burton advises potential bounty hunters to become friends with local precinct warrant officers, watch commanders, or men and women in the fugitive detail. They know who jumped bail. The watch commander is critical once the capture is made because the prisoner will be brought to her or his station. The processing and acknowledgment of the capture and claiming a reward occur at that juncture. Again, presenting yourself at the local police station, before the capture, is vital.

Bounty hunters taking people across state lines can encounter complicated and serious legal problems concerning the various state laws, constitutional issues, and private employee, employer, and prisoner rights. Once the person is captured, the bounty hunter returns the prisoner to the state from which he or she jumped bail. The bounty hunter is the surety's (bailbondsperson's [BBP's]) agent. Remanding the defendant for the reward is her/his only concern. Safe transport, violation of the person's rights, and constitutional issues are of limited relevance to the bounty hunter. Indeed, "federal constitutional provisions for extradition and the federal statutes implementing them are not intended primarily to safeguard the fugitive from justice, but rather to facilitate the discovery and bringing to speedy trial of fugitives from justice by the states."[6]

Keep in mind that bounty hunters work for bail bonds companies or themselves; that is, a law officer may have tipped them off about a fugitive. Perhaps the bounty hunter saw a wanted poster and decided the reward was worth the hunt. They are business people, with profit as their main objective. So there you have it. Essentially, the bounty hunter's and the law's interests are in closing the case, as well as protecting the surety's investment—bail. As explained previously, liberal provisions for the remission of forfeitures make it attractive for bondspersons to cover their losses by finding the defendant and returning the person for trial. Also, strict collection of bond correlates with deterrence against bail jumping.

To wit, bondspersons will spend time and money to find the skip, according to *Studies on Bail*, edited by Caleb Foote. Moreover, Foote assures us that bailbondspersons have police and underworld contacts. The latter group will likely cooperate with bailbondpeople in order to protect their own need for bail in the future.

The capture and return of a fugitive can be problematic for bounty hunters, especially when state lines are crossed. Prisoner safety during transport is unimportant. Anything can and sometimes does happen to the person being remanded. An article in the *San Diego Law Review* focused on prisoner extradition and transportation, as well as the power of a private agent conducting government activities, particularly when the prisoner had not been convicted of a crime. After a brief initial explanation about the defendant being raped and abused, those deeds were discussed in the context of topics listed above. Left unsaid was whether the transporting agents were charged and arrested, regarding injuring a prisoner. In actuality, the men were bounty hunters.[7]

Bail and Bailbondspersons

The current bail structure has its roots in English common law. It is a venerable and vigorous form of indemnity, which renders the guarantor liable to suffer any punishment the released prisoner has received. These private agents may or may not have had training nor are there universal qualifications. Neither training nor qualifications enter in any considerations about the best man or woman to bring the person back. In short, "the sureties can pursue the bonded person to other states and may even break and enter her or his house to effect arrest."[8]

Acting as a state's agent or law enforcement officer, "there's no need for search warrants or extradition papers."[9] Such limitless powers disregard the Constitution and Bill of Rights. Moreover, they can place all of us in danger if the reward is in the thousands. Granted, speedy trials are critical to our democracy. Still, violating a person's rights as well as abusing him or her is inexcusable in a democratic nation. Complicating matters, as noted, are the bail criminal codes that differ in every state. A brief examination of four states' process, beginning with Arizona, will be instructive. But first, more discussion of bail's history.

Perhaps the *Webster's Ninth New Collegiate Dictionary* (1991) definition of the two words will be useful: Bail, "security given for the due appearance of a prisoner in order to obtain his (her) release from imprisonment"; surety, "one who has become legally liable for the debt or default or failure in duty (as appearance in court) of another." (Surety or bailbondsperson can be used interchangeably.) In ancient England, the accused remained incarcerated until trial, thereby filling the jails. Designating someone to be responsible for the defendant's court appearance was the solution to overcrowding, as well as long imprisonment while awaiting a judge's arrival.

However, the bailbondsperson was completely responsible and liable for the accused, so much so that he served the defendant's sentence, including death, if the accused failed to keep his/her court date. Understandably, people were unhappy with taking the defendant's place in the criminal justice system and declined to be a surety. Subsequently, the law changed and a bond and/or collateral was posted guaranteeing that the defendant would face justice on the appointed date or forfeit the collateral. Further, the surety had complete rights concerning every aspect of the defendant's life and limb, including returning her or him to jail at will.

In other words, the accused's freedom from incarceration was supplanted by the stewardship of bail. By law, bailbondspersons can arrest their charge at any time, regardless of whether the person has violated the original bail contract. This surety can empower his or her agent, usually a bounty hunter, to effect the arrest. "By common law the bail has custody of the principal and [can] take him at any and in any place. The taking is not considered as the service process but a continuation of the custody committed to the bail. The principal may even be taken on Sunday, that day being considered a holy day. The dwelling house is no longer the castle of the principal in which he may place himself" to keep out of the bailbondsperson's reach (*Taylor v. Taintor* 16 Wall 366 [1873]).

"If the door should not be opened on demand at midnight, the Bailbondsman may break it down and take the principal from his bed, if that measure should be necessary to enable the Bailbondsman to take the principal" (*"Commonwealth* v. *Brickett"*). In short, "the giving of the recognizance by him only operated to transfer the custody of his person from the Sheriff to his sureties. Thenceforth, they, instead of the Sheriff, were his jailers. There was, therefore, no occasion for the issuance and service of a new order of arrest nor for a warrant of commitment" ("In Re: Henry Siebert," 112–16). Essentially, bounty hunters or any agent of the bailbondsperson, even you or I, can arrest, on instructions, a jumper or anyone out on bail.

Bob Burton opines that U.S. residents are amply protected from the state's massive coercive powers, but that we are less protected from one another. As is obvious from the preceding legal account, citizen's arrests occur daily with the full backing of common law. Societies are frequently defined by their monopoly of legitimate means of physical coercion. Throughout the nation's history there has been a shadow side of social control: vigilantes, a spontaneously organized posse, hate organizations, the bounty hunters, and other guns for hire, including private detectives. This tradition of the privatization of violence lives today. (See Tables 1.1, 1.2, and 1.3 for bail bond forms and surrendering defendant.)

Some of the reasons why bounty hunters choose this field were previously discussed. As unemployment soars, the suspicion is that the number of bounty hunters will increase. Few self-employed people have such minimal start-up costs, education requirements, or the need for licenses (except to carry a gun). Further, his/her power is enormous and exhilarating, and accountability is almost nil. With a $50 badge or

Table 1.1
Bail Bond Form

SAMPLE

State of New York)

               ss:

County of   )

    We the   , the surety mentioned in the annexed undertaking to answer, do hereby authorize and empower any policeman of the City of New York, or _____
_____
or either of them, in our name, place and stead, to take, seize and surrender the said _____
(in the said undertaking held as defendant) to the Court wherein he is bound to appear for trial, or deliver him to the custody of the authorities of said city and county; in our exoneration as surety therein.

Date _____, 19___

                                     {NAME OF SURETY}

              By _____
                              Attorney-in-Fact

a self-designed and developed business card and a gun, bounty hunters can (and do) force their way into a residence, capture someone on the street, and make citizen's arrests all with or without local law people and all very legal. Remember that bounty hunters' quasi legal standing at the time of capture stems from the auspices of a bondperson or surety company, operating under Article 4 of the U.S. Constitution and the February 12, 1793, authorization whereby bailbondspeople's jurisdiction is extended to their agent, a bounty hunter. This agent is hired to pursue and arrest a fleeing principal. Thus, a citizen's arrest is made without a warrant as we know it in the 1990s.

Table 1.2
Bail Bond Release Form

SAMPLE

BAIL BONDS

CONDITIONS OF RELEASE

Name _____

Address _____

City _____ State _____ Zip _____

Phone _____

****

The defendant, _____ as part of his/her bail must adhere to the following bail conditions. Failure to do so will result in revocation of the bail and the defendant returned to jail.

1. *You must report to our offices no later than twenty-four hours after your release from jail.*
2. *You will maintain contact with us once per week via telephone and/ or in person.*
3. *We must verify the address that you will be living at. (rent receipts, bills, mail, etc.)*
4. _____
5. _____

I the defendant _____ , do hereby agree to the following conditions of this release.

Despite a promising and steady downward trend as we enter the twenty-first century, crime is commonplace in the United States, from white collar and corporate crime to the violence of poverty. Still, in our democracy, efforts prevail that enable defendants, 65 percent of those facing felony charges,[10] to be released until trial, either through bail or on their own recognizance. The premise is that the accused can develop a stronger defense when he or she is free. To wit, "convicted defendants who had been detained until case disposition were twice as likely as released defendants to receive a state prison sentence,"[11] (see Tables 1.4 and 1.5 on adjudication outcome and sentencing outcome). In other words, "two-thirds of jailed defendants, until case disposition, were eventually convicted and sentenced to incarceration compared with

Table 1.3
Surrendering Defendant Form

SAMPLE

Date:

To whom it may concern:

I,   hereby authorize the bail enforcement agency
to act on my behalf in surrendering said defendant
back into custody.

I no longer wish to be the surety on this bail bond. I am exercising
my right to do so as per 530.80 of the CPL, State of New York.

                              signed

Notary

just a third of those released."[12] Now that the U.S. basis of hunting, capturing, and arresting people have been explained, we move to descriptions of bail in the four states targeted in this research.

Bail Laws

Arizona law is termed "simple and straightforward" concerning bail arrest. The precise law taken from the criminal code (#13–3885) describes the how to's and where for's of capturing a fugitive. As we discussed previously, for the purpose of surrendering the defendant, a bailbondsperson may arrest the fugitive before any forfeiture activities occur or by written authority. The latter must be endorsed on a certified copy of the undertaking, thereby empowering any adult person of suitable discretion to do so.[13]

New Jersey's bail law provides defendants a chance to turn themselves in "but such render shall be made within twenty days after proceeding or an action is commenced against the bail on the recognizance of bail and not after."[14] It is hoped that defendants are given the twenty day's benefit. Knowing one's bail arrests rights are key. Furthermore, bounty hunters must learn the principle tenets of bail law for every state in which they operate. Ignorance of the law can cost a bounty hunter the reward.

Table 1.4
Median Bail Amount, 1990

Most serious arrest charge	Median bail amount for felony defendants		Most serious arrest charge	Median bail amount for felony defendants	
	Released	Detained		Released	Detained
All offenses	$3,000	$7,500	Drug offenses	$5,000	$5,000
Violent offenses	$5,000	$10,000			
			Sales/trafficking	3,500	8,500
Murder	10,000	50,000	Other drug	5,000	5,000
Rape	10,000	20,000			
Robbery	5,000	10,000	Public-order offenses	$2,500	$7,500
Assault	3,000	10,000			
Other violent	5,000	15,000	Driving-related	2,500	10,000
Property offenses	$2,500	$5,000	Other public order	2,000	5,500
Burglary	3,000	7,500			
Theft	2,500	5,000	Note: Table includes only defendants for whom a bail amount was set.		
Other property	2,500	5,000			

Source: U.S. Department of Justice, "National Pretrial Reporting Program: Pretrial Release of Felony Defendants," *Bureau of Justice Statistics Bulletin* (1990).

New Mexico, too, allows for a bondsperson to be relieved of the bail bond obligation, even though the person may not be violating the terms of the bail. Therefore, "the surety may arrest the accused and deliver him to the Sheriff of the county in which the action against the accused is pending."[15] Proper documentation of the bail order and bond are required at all times. Here again knowledge of bail arrest laws are critical to the accused.

Last, New York has a specific stipulation about bail: "at any time before the forfeiture of a bail bond an obligor may surrender the defendant in his exoneration, or the defendant may surrender himself to the court . . . or to the Sheriff."[16] Even a cursory examination of bail laws in a given state illustrates this feature's critical importance. The average man or woman's conception of bail is freedom for an accused person until trial, provided the person remains in town. Rescinding the defendant's bail without her/him having violated the rules is a foreign notion. Yet, this process occurs frequently, and incarceration is always imminent.

For example, when interviewing a bail enforcement agent (the interviewee preferred that term), we were interrupted by a bailbondsperson requesting assistance in rescinding bail. I listened while a fee was negotiated and arrangements made to "bring the person in." The bail enforcement agent later explained that the surety suspected the person "might jump bail," and decided protecting his collateral was more important than the defendant's freedom. Further, the bondsper-

Table 1.5
Speed of Adjudication, 1990

Detention/release outcome and most serious original arrest charge	Felony defendants in the 75 largest counties							
	Number of de- fendants	Median number of days	Percent of cases adjudicated within					Percent not adjudicated within 1 year
			1 week	1 month	3 months	6 months	1 year	
Released defendants								
All offenses	35,398	125	2%	15%	40%	63%	81%	19%
Violent offenses	8,764	131	2	15	39	61	81	19
Property offenses	12,152	116	2	16	42	66	82	18
Drug offenses	11,639	138	2	12	38	59	80	20
Public-order offenses	2,843	105	1	17	47	71	86	14
Detained defendants								
All offenses	19,628	37	12%	45%	73%	89%	96%	4%
Violent offenses	5,343	66	9	33	59	80	91	9
Property offenses	6,463	30	14	50	79	93	98	2
Drug offenses	6,512	35	14	47	78	91	98	2
Public-order offenses	1,309	30	9	50	79	91	98	2

Note: Data on time from arrest to adjudication were available for 97% of all adjudicated cases. Because of violation of the conditions of release (such as failure to appear in court or rearrest), 12% of the defendants who had been on pretrial release were in custody at the time of adjudication. These defendants are included under "released." The median for time from arrest to adjudication includes cases still pending at the end of the study. Knowing the exact times for these cases would not change the medians reported.

Source: U.S. Department of Justice, "National Pretrial Reporting Program: Pretrial Release of Felony Defendants," *Bureau of Justice Statistics Bulletin* (1990).

son preferred hiring a bail enforcement agent rather than doing the work himself.

Giving and then taking away a person's freedom is almost like playing God. Some argue it is reprehensible. After all, U.S. justice provides that one is innocent until proven guilty. But the media reports so much information regarding a suspect's background, police record (if any), mug shots, as well as the capture that guilt is often assumed. In any event, the suspect has the right to request bail. Whether it is granted depends on various things including the nature of the crime and previous record. Paramount in the judge's decision is community safety. Affordability is critical for the defendant.

Questions regarding bail are numerous and complex. Putting the community's safety ahead of freeing a suspect makes sense. However, a legal issue surfaces: preventive detention, that is, locking up people to protect the community in advance of conviction or until proven innocent. This issue flies in the face of precedents that the only requirement is ensuring the defendants' appearance at his/her trial. The preventive detention practice has close ties with totalitarianism. It endangers democratic principles and rule by law. The Constitution's Eighth Amendment stipulates that "excessive bail shall not be required."

Admittedly, the amendment failed to say that bail should be set in every case. Former New York City judge Bruce Wright is an example of public controversy over bail. He was soundly criticized by law enforcement officers because he adhered to the Constitution by requiring bail that people could afford or by releasing them on their own recognizance. Consequently, officials nicknamed him "Turn-em-loose Bruce." In general, pejoratives are seldom used against judges, even those who set bail for organized crime members when none is warranted. However, in the 1990s criticisms against the judiciary by prosecutors and politicians are mounting. Such overt affronts were unusual responses and were also disrespectful. Few spoke out in Wright's defense, as far as can be determined. For more information about Bruce Wright's judicial experiences and the bail, read his book *Black Robes, White Justice*.

Where does the bounty hunter fit in the bail issue? On the side of bail enforcement. Once bail is granted to a suspect, he or she represents potential employment for bounty hunters. They are the enforcement arm of the bailbond system. Under these circumstances, younger bounty hunters prefer the designation bail enforcement agent. Expanded preventive detentions or incarcerations due to dire economic straits could mean less need for BEAs. However, concern about the bail enforcement agents' plight is premature. So many people are arrested that bail enforcement agents/bounty hunters can even afford to provide employment for others. An internship or partnership with an experienced bounty hunter in charge is often the norm in densely populated urban East Coast areas. Moreover, many bounty hunters are private investigators, finding runaway spouses (just as they did in colonial times), among other assignments. Additional details are in the history section.

Bail laws, clarified previously, differ by state; in fact within a state, discrepancies exist. New York City is a case in point. A New York City Police Department *Legal Bureau Bulletin* makes clear that "courts have traditionally afforded the bondsman an absolute right to apprehend the defendants; without a warrant or court process."[17] Yet, at the conclusion it is noted that "Bondsmen will not be permitted to break and enter a premises for the purpose of arresting a defendant inside."[18]

In other words, bondspersons or their agents can apprehend a person without any arrest warrant. However, apprehension is predicated on refraining from breaking and entering the premises. Some bounty hunters flaunt the law concerning these constraints. Seemingly, as we have read, this action is backed up by the U.S. Supreme Court. Peter Moses, author of an article in the *New York Post*, April 9, 1989, entitled "Little Lynette Bounty Hunter," featured a twenty-five-year-old female bounty hunter. Moses said, "Bounty Hunters occupy an interesting niche in the criminal justice system. They can legally knock down a door in pursuit of a 'skip' as long as they have an arrest warrant." The previous sentence would lead most readers to conclude that bailbondspersons or their agents in New York are issued arrest warrants by police that legally permit breaking and entering residences. In reality, the bail bond contract acts as private warrant to apprehend defendants without breaking and entering. Other states may or may not have the same restrictions.

Remember, the *Legal Bureau Bulletin* noted that a warrant is unnecessary, but breaking and entering is not permitted. Bail enforcement agent Harry showed me a copy of the U.S. Supreme Court decision almost every bounty hunter or bail enforcement agent carries on his or her person. This decision legitimizes and authorizes bounty hunter's work. It stipulates in part, "Whenever they choose to do so, they may seize and deliver him up in their charge, and if that cannot be done at once they may imprison him until it can be done." In addition, just like in seventeenth-century England, they "may break and enter his house for that purpose [of making an arrest]."[19] Contradictions aside, lay people might wonder why a search warrant, together with an arrest warrant, are unnecessary?

Money is the root of the problem. In a capitalist society, this is unsurprising. To wit, a bailbondsperson promises to pay the local or federal government a sum of money, fixed by the court, regarding a person charged with a crime. Should the defendant flee or fail to keep his/her court appearance, the bondsperson can do everything necessary to minimize his/her losses, all in the guise of swift justice. New York City bail enforcement agent Harry (not his name) explains the process of apprehension, including knocking down a suspect's door, without warrants: "Notify the local precinct, describe the surveillance team and their vehicle, request police back-up when actual arrest is made." Police may decide against assisting bailbondspersons or their agents and are not compelled to do so.

During capture, the bounty hunter must provide the following identification: a certified copy of the bail bond, written notarized authorization from the bailbondsperson, and a forfeiture notice. Bounty hunters and/or BEAs are required by law to show these items to the police when requesting back-up. (You may recall from the earlier story about Annette, identification was not furnished.) In conclusion, Harry cautions that a defendant's identity must be established beyond any doubt, matching New York State identification member (NYSID) and the National Crime Information Center (NCIC) computer at the Federal Bureau of Investigation headquarters.

Thinking people recoil at the fact that armed civilians without warrants can break in a residence and remove the occupant. For these civilians, some of whom are former police officers, accountability, supervision, or training are minimal to nonexistent. Presumably injuries and mistakes can and do occur. What recourse do people have when the court extends its full authority to civilians, thus privatizing an act that is democracy's foundation? A worse case scenario is that the "jumper" will be killed.

True, agrees Harry solemnly, but the death of a jumper is unlikely since it requires too much paperwork as well as a legal hearing. These procedures cost the bounty hunter time and money, and he/she risks prison or a lawsuit. Still a bounty hunter will get paid for bringing back the bail jumper "dead or alive." The latter issue is discussed in the 1800s section. Note the terminology used here: Dead is mentioned first. If police officers and bounty hunters arrive simultaneously to arrest a fugitive and someone is injured or killed, police officers control the situation and are ultimately responsible, notes bounty hunter Bob Burton. Let us continue examining the employers of bounty hunters.

Surety Companies/Bailbondspersons in New York City

Most people would argue that BBPs provide a community service. They ensure an accused freedom while awaiting trial. Recently, in summer 1996, CNN and other news stations reported results of an occupational survey that noted bailbondsmen and -women were in the nation's second most dangerous profession, and as such, were second most likely to be killed. Taxi drivers were in first place. Indeed, these entrepreneurs maintain the vitality and validity of the presumption that everyone is innocent until proved guilty. Further, the literature suggests there is minimal chance a surety company will lose money bailing a person out of jail because most defendants keep their court dates.

In addition, the company requires two cosigners and collateral from the defendants' family or friends, usually 10 percent of bail, as well as strict daily telephone or in-person communication by the accused. New York City, for instance, has a strict bail collections procedure. Thus, surety companies have an incentive to keep track of the accused or spend their own money and time to capture and return a bail jumper for trial. Knowing apprehension is inevitable can act as a deterrent, since bounty hunters or bail enforcers will pursue a fugitive across state lines, even to other nations.

According to knowledgeable sources, bail jumpers receive little or no attention from the police; actually, police give bounty hunters information on skips and appear only during capture, if then. Pursuing bail jumpers is extremely time consuming and a fruitless endeavor. If the jumper leaves the state or area, police officers are virtually out of the picture. Bounty hunters can and do cross state lines and, as has been explained, are bound by very few rules. This lack of concern by the police department operates on behalf of the bounty hunters, keeping them employed. Hence, the bounty hunter captures and returns a person for a bounty, and if acquainted with local police personnel, will receive credit for a "collar." Collar refers to an arrest. The term reflects that, in a past era, the public's image of being arrested was the officer grabbing the person by his or her collar and taking them to jail.

Local police recognition lends an air of respectability to bounty hunters. It is a door opener; news of the credited arrest spreads through the law enforcement grapevine and both surety company and bounty hunter gain. The jumper is back in custody without considerable loss to the company, and the bounty hunter receives a hefty fee, increased validity, and respect. Burton comments that bounty hunters and the bail bond industry recapture 80 percent of skips. The remaining 20 percent are not caught by BEAs. These fugitives surrender, are captured during routine traffic stops, or are never apprehended. The average bounty hunter arrest costs $800, while it costs hundreds, if not thousands, of taxpayer dollars, notes Burton, to effectuate a capture by municipal police. They arrest less than 22 percent of fugitives. These private sector bounty hunters, bail enforcement agents, and bailbondspersons cost the public nothing. A description of the actual bail process is provided in subsequent paragraphs.

The Bail Process

The surety company, with its state required financial resources, can (and do) attain critical importance to the defendant at the arrest-imprisonment stage. Usually a female relative or friend contacts the company regarding bail. If the collateral requirements are met, along with written assurances concerning keeping in touch with the bailbondsperson, then the man or woman is released. In the twentieth century bailbondspersons' businesses have diversified. They are partners with private detective agencies or the reverse, providers of bail enforcement agents and bounty hunters. Also, some of the companies serve legal papers, find missing persons, collect divorce evidence, and furnish bodyguards. Insurance fraud investigation is another vital component of these agencies' services, together with undercover activities. However, bail enforcement agents/bounty hunters have a major role in the bailbondspersons' companies.

Significantly, New York City has just four bail bondspersons, according to a Bronx, New York, bailbondsman John Smith (alias) in a telephone interview. From nearly two hundred to just five bailbondspersons in the four boroughs; one each in Brooklyn, the Bronx, and Staten Island, and two in Queens. Legislation in the 1960s put bailbondspersons out of business, says Smith. He attributed that phenomenon to low bail, pretrial services, release on own recognizance, summonses, and the government's quick collection of defaulted bonds when the accused failed to appear in court. "There are no bail bondspersons from the Bronx, New York, line to Canada," said Smith. He believes judges are foolhardy to release people charged with crimes without the restraint of a bailbondsperson.

Nevertheless, judges must abide by the law under the Bail Reform Act of 1984. Pretrial release is required and, according to section 3142-B, "the defendant must be on prerecognition or unsecured bond unless the judicial officer determines that such release will not reasonably assure the appearance of the person as required, or will endanger the safety of any other person or the community. Release is always subject to the condition that the person not commit a federal, state or local crime during the period of release."[20] Presumably the accused will refrain from absconding given the likelihood of being rearrested or living as a fugitive. Further, bail jumping is a separate (additional) offense, as noted in the *Federal Bail and Detention Handbook*, by the Honorable John L. Weinberg, United States Magistrate, Practicing Law Institute, 1994.

Actually, "approximately one in four released defendants had a bench warrant issued for their arrest because they did not appear in court as scheduled."[21] The foregoing numbers support bounty hunters' and their advocates' contention that thousands of fugitives are at large. Thus bounty hunters/bail enforcement agents perform a vital community service, remanding the criminals to prison. Bail or personal release are hotly debated, with sharply drawn lines by voters on either side of the debate. A discussion of the issue in this book is too complex and extensive to address. Having become acquainted with their employers, a discussion about the company bounty hunters keep is in the subsequent paragraphs.

Motivating the bounty hunter/bail enforcement agent's actions, that is, returning as many skips as possible, are profits. They are business people, and more captures mean more money. Collecting the numerous rewards can foster very comfortable lifestyles. Who are these people? Developing a typical profile is nearly impossible, but some consistent characteristics among bail enforcement agents and bounty hunters do emerge. A brief review of an average bounty hunter's background in the context of employment opportunities in the 1990s yields interesting information.

Bounty Hunters' Background

The white male participation rate in the U.S. civilian labor force has declined from 80 percent in 1970 to 76 percent in 1992. Those remaining and entering the work force must have a high school diploma. Often firms want employees that have one or two years of college or even undergraduate and graduate degrees. Obviously, such requirements exclude a number of people from gainful employment. Regional and state reviews are instructive. In the northeast, 74 percent of all civilian males in 1992 were employed; with 9 percent unemployed, the number decreases a percentage point each in New York, New Jersey, and Pennsylvania. Improved employment prospects for underskilled workers are unlikely given the proliferation of part-time, no benefits, low-wage jobs.

The lack of formal qualifications means that bounty hunting is a near perfect profession, attracting diverse people. Concomitantly, the glamour, excitement, and self-direction must be acknowledged as additional drawing cards to the profession.

Moreover, the legal use of high-tech, state-of-the-art weapons are the ultimate attraction. Unfortunately, such devices can draw people who should not have access to weapons or the ability to obtain confidential information. In other words, these instruments in the wrong hands can endanger everyone's lives.

Surveillance on cheating spouses, insurance investigations, and security checks (on potential mates and for employment purposes) are special assignments that local law enforcement officials cannot handle (due to legal constraints and lack of personnel). These are the continuing and burgeoning jobs that bounty hunters/bail enforcement agents do for handsome fees. Bail enforcement is increasingly a less important feature in the bounty hunters' repertoire. They have diversified with a vengeance. Given these circumstances and the unfortunate economic situation for the majority of people, it is likely that the number of bounty hunters will increase in proportion to crime and required sentencing. In this quickly expanding industry, they are vital partners to the nation's criminal justice institution and prison-industrial complex in the twentieth and twenty-first centuries. As befitting all business persons, these professionals are employing modern technology in their daily business activities.

Tools of the Trade

For the foreseeable future, bounty hunting is here to stay, differing from its ancient antecedents only by the availability of high-tech weapons, telephone books, and computers. Monetary rewards to find all kinds of people for various reasons will likely always have a major role in our society and similar ones. A case in point, commissioning tax bounty hunters is a time-honored practice by the government who uses lawyers "to ferret out and collect taxes from those allegedly owing taxes . . . in the state."[22] New Jersey engaged the services of the Municipal Tax Bureau, owned by an attorney, "a reputed tax commando."[23] Presumably, the bounty is on a percentage performance basis.

Another example is that, in early 1996, among the hundreds of rewards offered internationally in every area of human interaction, $2 million was posted for the return of a terrorist who escaped from prison in Italy. He was captured quickly, but it is unknown whether the reward was paid. In any event, we have witnessed in the 1990s a vast collection of data that yielded extensive personal information on most U.S residents. Bounty hunters and other agents have taken advantage of this situation, through computer software purchases or knowing people with easy or restricted data access. Ominously, confidentiality and privacy are anachronisms heralding a major blow to democracy. In fact, one bounty hunter told me it is easier than ever to find someone. He said a computer cuts the work in half, using the right programs, one can let the fingers do the walking, especially when one knows an individual's social security number.

Aside from a computer, the telephone and family are the next best avenues for capturing a fugitive. Further, there are magazines, even the bounty hunter newsletter, *Hunters' Net*, offering a range of services and advertisements from up-to-date legal notes and weapons to notices of rewards for unsolved crimes. *National Crime Reporter's* lead article, in May 1978, entitled "Bounty Hunter's Delight," discussed outstanding rewards and proclaimed that a "secret witness army" was being mobilized to help police fight crime. *Hunter's Net*, the voice of the American bounty hunter, has articles that run the gamut on information from Arizona's bill that "seeks proof that bail funds are legally acquired" to an article against gun control. In addition there are advertisements by private investigators and for international fugitive recovery, pepper foam, as well as Smith and Wesson handcuffs.

That bounty hunters and bail enforcement agents carry such weapons are of major concern to the local crime fighters: "their services are not always welcomed by law enforcement officials, many of whom think Bounty Hunters routinely abuse their authority to make arrests," says

Timothy M. Ito (54). Notwithstanding that issue, bounty hunters feel they must use every possible avenue in their work because, as explained previously, they have a limited time frame in which to make the capture before the bail is forfeited (Burton, "An Interview"). Despite this effort, a bailbondsperson sometimes does not pay the bounty hunter/bail enforcement agent expeditiously. There may be two or three days', even a week's, delay due to insurance issues or regular business practice. But in the 1800s, bounty hunters were paid immediately, with some exceptions, whether the fugitive was dead or alive. More details are provided in the 1800s section (see pages 35–44).

Female Bounty Hunters

In the twentieth century, women are in the bounty hunting profession. Carolyn Kelley, a bounty hunter and the first woman of African descent to be a bailbondsperson in New Jersey, believes women make excellent bounty hunters. Kelley observes that capturing the fugitive is easier since few men feel threatened by women, nor do they expect a bounty hunter to be female. Consequently, male fugitives are less likely to suspect that a woman is tracking him. Once the fugitive is confronted, comments Kelley, they rarely resist arrest. (See the full account on Kelley and Baird on pages 25–35.)

In New Mexico, Teri Baird is Kelley's counterpart, having been in the bail bond and bounty hunting business for twenty years. Baird entered the profession through her father; the current business is family owned and staffed. In the 1990s, at least 50 percent of bailbondspersons are women, according to Baird. She is frustrated by the unsavory image of bounty hunters and bailbondspersons. Baird thinks strict licensing and enforcement will promote a more respectable reputation for these two professions. Indeed, ten years ago New Mexico instituted bail bond licensing and classes; the latter are ongoing and, says Baird, must be completed yearly for legal updates.

New Jersey, with its bailbondspersons numbering in the hundreds, also has licensing under the state insurance department (as do Arizona, New Mexico, and New York). Lynette Shaw "works for the bounty hunting unit of her father's bail bonding firm. She became enamored with the business at the age of 13 when her father let her tag along with Bounty Hunters."[24] Presumably, a child (is) was the perfect ruse when stalking a fugitive. Notice that two of the women came into the profession through family connections.

All in all, it is a difficult business, especially when hunting bail *skips* without connections. As was made clear in preceding sections, law enforcement and personal connections are crucial to success. You will see these same relationships in the chapter on city marshals. Kelley's law enforcement connection was her background as a corrections officer. The closeness of municipal police officers, sheriffs or city marshals, bailbondspersons, and bounty hunters is apparent. Whether this bond between government law enforcement and private business should be encouraged or eliminated is an important issue that requires public visibility and discussion on a national level.

Interviews with Bounty Hunters and Bailbondpersons

Edited Telephone Interview: Bob Burton

When that person takes out a bail bond, they waive their rights. On the other hand, we are pretty helpless against a large police force. But there are various laws to protect us against each other. A bounty hunter can definitely arrest without a warrant and can cross states' lines and can enter their home. We have the right to make these arrests because the bond applicant, now fugitive, agrees to the rules. This does not cost taxpayers a dime, that is, a bonding agent is paying me to do a job. The bail bonds industry as a whole gets 80 percent of people that jump bail, the other 13 percent are caught or surrender during routine traffic stops. It costs over $800 to arrest a criminal according to the National Institute of Justice. The average big city police department catches less than 12 to 22 percent of their fugitives. We Bounty Hunters have the best incentive to engage in a pursuit. No body, no booty. We are the private sector. Security is given to a bailbondsperson for the due appearance of a prisoner in order to obtain his or her release from imprisonment. A bailbondsperson is one who becomes legally liable for the debt or default or failure in duty [as appearance in court] of another. In conclusion, police and bounty hunter often arrive simultaneously, the former as a back-up to keep the peace. But if local police get a call about the same fugitive and respond, a bounty hunter will still get paid. Nevertheless, in cases of a serious offender, municipal police will assume full control. Again, a bounty hunter will still get paid. Some states, Texas and Massachusetts, will issue the bounty hunters a warrant for the arrest.

Edited Telephone Interview: Stan Rifkin, Bounty Hunter

I was raised in a New York City orphanage. From nine to nineteen years old it was my home in Westchester. My mother was from Russia and worked in sweatshops for twenty-five cents an hour. She visited me every Sunday. I used to trap muskrats and beavers to sell for fur and plowed fields with a tractor at nine years old. I taped two-by-fours to pedals in order to drive a tractor for plowing. Also, I lived in Home

Crest in Yonkers, a Hebrew National Orphanage, where I helped cook. I left there for the Marines, where I did undercover work in the brig in order to determine maltreatment by prison guards. I have one sister, much older, and a brother who died in July 1995. My first wife died; I now have a second wife and son. My hobbies include skin diving, fishing, roller skating, and ballroom dancing competition.

I have been a professional bounty hunter forty-one years. I am one of two bounty hunters in the country or world for the last twenty-five years. There have been documentaries and a movie on me: *The Hunter*, starring Steve McQueen. Robert DeNiro rode with me for the bounty hunter movie, *Midnight Run*. I began my bounty hunter career with finance companies. For a year I was a skip tracer at $45 a week. In 1955, a bailbondsperson phoned concerning a skip, and offered me twenty-five bucks to pick up the fugitive. [Skip refers to a person out on bail who does not return for a court appearance.]

This bailbondsperson told me how to go about getting the man, then asked me whether I wanted to be a bounty hunter. Technically, as a novice, I couldn't go outside the area. According to a 1892 federal decision, when bail is given, the principal is regarded as a continuance. Thus, he/she (bailbondsperson) can exercise his or her rights to retrieve a defendant. No due process is needed. The person on bail is still a prisoner. A bailbondsperson can take him back to prison at anytime. But, neither a bailbondsperson or bounty hunter is considered a peace-officer. Furthermore, the bounty hunter needs a certified copy of the bail bond. This "surrender piece" [bail bond] becomes a so-called warrant, according to 530.80 criminal procedure law, New York State penal code.

Anybody above the age of twenty, provided he/she has the original receipt of bail, can pick up a person. A skip tracer working for one company in New York state does not need a license. But every state is different. Florida says you need a runners license. Furthermore, the bounty hunter must present and have a bailbondsperson license. I do all the work myself. In New York state, a bounty hunter has a year to bring back the person; then a motion must be clocked in before the year is up. Specifically, the motion to vacate the forfeiture before the year ends is required. Once bail is forfeited, it goes to the district attorney and then to the bailbondsperson's insurance company.

New York state counties refused to exonerate the bail, and they started charging interest on the bail, 9 percent. Their actions drove the bailbondsperson out of business. Ten to 15 percent is allowed on bail-bonds fees in other states. For most of the fees, the state insurance department handles them. The bailbondsperson must find an insurance company who will provide a [bond] power of $10,000, $15,000 or more. Thus the bailbondsperson can write a bond up to that amount. An insurance company must back a bailbondsperson or he/she will not get his license. Bailbondsperson's fees are regulated by the insurance company. It gets all the fees at the end of the month, and then said company returns a certain percentage of fees to a bailbondsperson. The higher the bond, the more money for the bailbondsperson and insurance company, as well as contributions for a "build-up" fund to help bailbondspersons after they retire.

Many states have a prerelease system which entails a $5,000 surety or $1,000 in cash. It is easier to put up collateral. An indemnifier signs for the bail bonds, that is, he/she signs for the bail and/or puts up collateral. Most bailbondspersons demand two indemnifiers. Collateral is returned if the person appears in court at the designated time. If he/she jumps bail [fails to appear], the indemnifier will have to pay all fees, including the bounty hunter, as well as the balance of the bond. I have lectured to many classes in criminal justice on this subject. Bounty hunting is a dangerous job. Drugs and illegal aliens make the job more dangerous. People are desperate either to make money or live in the United States. Still, the most dangerous bounty hunter, jobs are mob related.

I am not as busy as in the past, since bailbondspersons are not needed as in earlier days, because people are released on their own recognizance. Bounty hunters receive a percentage of the total amount of the bail bond and expenses [each case is different]. This includes car rentals, informants fees [biggest expense], phone calls, airfare, food, hotel. There are about seven hundred to one thousand bounty hunters all over the country. Most are ex-sheriffs or cops.

Marshals, warrant squads, fugitive squads, and sheriffs provide information about skips, such as his or her previous history. Normally, people go back to their old stomping grounds, like the same barber. Also, bounty hunters must know the nature of the crime and should interview the arresting cops. At one time, I had a motor home with a cell built inside and a special license plate that announced my occupation and name, Bounty Hunter Rifkin.

Edited Excerpts of an Interview: Carolyn Kelley—Newark, New Jersey, Bailbondsperson and Bounty Hunter

JP: I'm speaking with Ms. Carolyn Kelley this morning. She describes her background.

Kelley: My name is Carolyn Kelley. I was born and raised in Newark, New Jersey. Early on I decided to become involved with politics because I saw how black people lived, and I decided I wanted to help make a difference. After getting involved in politics, since I wasn't able to go to school to become a lawyer, I decided to become a bailbondsagent. After graduating from bail bonds school in 1971, I became the first black female bailbondsagent or bailbondsperson in the state of New Jersey.

JP: Where?

Kelley: The school I went to was in Irvington, New Jersey. That was in 1971. And the courses, I recall, were maybe one hundred hours. That's the easiest part.

JP: Is the school still there?

Kelley: No, it's not there any longer. There are some, though, still in the state, but that particular one isn't there. Bailbondspersons are licensed by the state. The first thing you have to do is go to one of those private schools and pass the test. Then you pass a state test.

JP: You know which department of state administers the test?

Kelley: Insurance.

JP: And does the insurance department issue the license?

Kelley: Yes, the department of insurance within the state. They issue one's license.

JP: When does the license expire?

Kelley: In a year.

JP: Is there a charge for the license?

Kelley: It started out $30. It's about $50 now.

JP: Describe your responsibilities.

Kelley: Let's say a woman has been arrested and charged for aggravated assault. Aggravated assault means you have used a weapon, something other than your hands or in addition to your hands. Let's say, hypothetically, her bail is $5,000. What she has to pay is 10 percent of that $5,000, which would be $500 cash. But she also has to have at least $2,500 in collateral. Now that collateral could either be in property, which I usually discourage people from pledging because traditionally the bailbondsagents will find a way, once the prisoner doesn't return to court, to take that property. So I often discourage that.

JP: As a bailbondswoman, you discourage that practice?

Kelley: Oh, yes. I've even had a few get out of jail on credit, which means, nine times out of ten, you don't get paid. But again it's in keeping with a bigger picture. That bigger picture was in pulling that person out of that jail cell. It has also always been very interesting to me that in all the crime and all the people in the United States of America, 85 to 89 percent are black and/or Hispanic. They talk about rehabilitation. There is absolutely no such animal as rehabilitation in the prison system here in the state of New Jersey.

Kelley: To strip a man or woman of any pride, any self-respect, any self-worth, any self-esteem, it's sad. I have had situations where people have been arrested. I'll give you one in particular. This man he was arrested, and his family sent for me. Now the third person acts as an indemnitor for the person who has been arrested. In other words, that indemnitor is responsible for either returning that person to court on his/her due date or they will then forfeit whatever collateral they have put up.

JP: Who are the two people? You said the third person is the indemnitor?

Kelley: Well, the first person is the person who is incarcerated. The second person is myself. The third person is the person who's coming to me to act as a responsible person or the indemnitor.

JP: So that would be the prisoner, you, and a family member?

Kelley: Exactly. A family member, girlfriend, close friend, minister. I remember this case in particular where this man had been arrested, and I went up to the cell block to see him and, of course, to get the particulars from him—how old he was, where was he born, who would act as the indemnitor, or where did he know he could put his hands on some money. And there's a retainer. The retainer had an FOA [For Other Authorities], meaning, for example, he had committed a crime in New York. So, there would be an FOA on him for New York, which means then, once I effectuate his release in the state of New Jersey, he still wasn't free to go because he owes the state of New York for whatever that crime is. And in this case they had an FOA for South Carolina. So, I went to him and said what could that be so that I could then contact South Carolina and possibly get it removed or resolved, whatever way is necessary. And he said "Ms. Kelley, I haven't been in South Carolina since I was three years old." I said, "Three years old? I don't understand." So, after talking to him I looked at the paperwork, and I saw this particular detective had put the retainer on. So I said, "Do you know him, or is this the arresting officer?" He said, "Miss, I'm a pimp. My girls were on the street, and the police officer wanted to go to bed with someone without paying and I refused." And so he put an FOA on him. Well, I went down to this detective and said how dare you, how dare you.

JP: You confronted him?

Kelley: Oh, yes, I did. Because, you see, once I'm putting my money up, actually submitting a promissory note to the court, saying that I'm responsible for that individual. That means that he's their prisoner, but he's my client. I'm acting on his behalf. I said how dare you? You will either produce proof that this man committed a crime in South Carolina at the age of three or I'm going to see your boss. I'm going to the police chief. He took it off naturally. That man hasn't spoken to me in about fifteen years.

I've seen women in the cell. Officers forced them to have sex for a cigarette or a candy bar, or to make a telephone call. I've had mothers have heart attacks seeing their sons in handcuffs. It's a traumatic experience seeing your child taken away from you, I don't care how old that child is. And you have no control over it. They have what they call here a sweep in Essex County, and that's usually twice a year. I would dare say it's in early November and somewhere around June or July, and they just round up people.

So, I studied the situation concerning the high numbers of blacks and Latinos behind bars, and I found that here's a black prisoner and here's a white one. Their entire background could be the same, no previous arrest, for example, graduated school, committed the one crime. But I always find that white man's bail would be much lower than the black male. I mean, such a decided difference even Ray Charles or Stevie Wonder could see it. Consequently, I would interview with them saying I'm going to make a difference in your life. I'm going to get you out of jail on bail, and if you don't pay me I'm going to find you and break your neck. Everybody has paid me except this one particular guy who looked at me real strange and said where did this jerk come from. And I said to him, "Do you understand I will physically break your neck if you don't give me my money?" "Oh yes, yes, yes sister. Oh, thank you, thank you." Sure enough, everybody came back except him.

JP: Did you trust him when you two first met?

Kelley: Intuitively no, and my gut instinct always prevails, so I watched him. Actually, I always find out where my clients' hang out and the areas they mostly frequent. This particular guy hung out in a bar down Broad Street. Well, I waited two days and he didn't show up.

Kelley: See, being a black woman in this business gives me a silent advantage because in this sense, they never expect me to do the same thing. See they call this, number one, a man's world.

JP: So what are some of the advantages?

Kelley: The advantage of, for example, I bail men out of jail and they jump bail on me. One man in particular I went looking for him in a bar also. He had clearly jumped bail. And I said to him when he saw me, "You don't think I bailed you out just because you have a problem in New York?" He said, "Uh, what?" I said, "I thought we could do something else." Well, he flew out that bar, got in my car, I locked him in, I didn't stop driving 'til I was on the sidewalk of the fourth precinct in Newark. When I arrived at the precinct, I just started blowing horn, I drove right up on the sidewalk, and by the time he could get himself together, the police were out there, and there he was locked up. There is another advantage. Because they're looking at you, number one, they think you're dumb; number two, because you're black, you just can't have good sense at all; and then being a female, they think it's a sexual thing or that it can end up being a sexual thing when in fact all I have on my mind is getting them out of jail so that they can fight for themselves, defend themselves so to speak.

JP: Why is that so important to get them out?

Kelley: Because behind bars you can't do anything for yourself. You're stripped of everything that has to do with this civilization. You can only make a phone call when they let you. And you can't make but so many of them. You have to call collect. Some people have blocks on their phones, some people don't even have phones.

JP: Why do you have to call collect?

Kelley: Because you can't have money on you. Prisoners don't have money. Once you are arrested, arresting officers place your personal property in a brown bag or manila envelope, give you a receipt and lock your personal belongings up. Consequently, if you had jewelry and/or money, upon release, you probably will never see the item again. A lot of times when they're arrested like that they don't sign anything or itemize things or identify what their personal property is. They're so nervous, state of shock, or whatever. Some are high on drugs, so the procedures just get right by them. And that's to the advantage of the person who sign for the items. However, you'll find some police officers who are really human beings. The black ones I have found to be worse. I have found the black ones to be absolutely the most disgusting things you've ever seen. The black police officers seem to feel that they have to prove something to white America. It's sad.

JP: What did you do before you became a bailbondsperson?

Kelley: I was employed at Caldwell Penitentiary for approximately two years as a correctional officer. I stayed in trouble up there. Every other month I was being suspended. For example, one girl said to me, "I haven't had peanut butter and jelly in years. Please see if you can get me some peanut butter and jelly." And that stayed on my mind the whole weekend. Didn't I go to the store and buy a bottle of peanut butter and a jar of jelly? I purchased glass jars instead of plastic. Naturally, the sergeant wanted to know which officer brought that in? How did she get that? No one sent anything. Knowing she was going to punish everybody, I couldn't let that happen. She gave me two weeks suspension without pay.

JP: Were you the only black person?

Kelley: There were three of us.

JP: Would you say that the prison system, in terms of guards, are mainly white?

Kelley: Predominantly white, yes. But the inmates are predominantly black. That's why they're building so many new ones now. It's big business. They make all the license plates for every car you see. And they're trying to pass a bill to make them pay for their own medical expenses. They do all the laundry for the hospitals. They do all the laundry in the state for $40 a month. And then they buy their toothpaste, tooth brushes, deodorant, et cetera.

JP: How and why are you so political with your background in enforcement?

Kelley: Well, maybe because of the kind of mother and father who raised me and my two brothers. They taught me all through life about my blackness. They shared with me and indoctrinated me with never to want to be other than myself. They taught me that as long as I have a brother or sister in the gutter, so was I. My father used to always say, "Carolyn, if a man or woman is in a hospital or in jail, if you don't help them then, they won't need you at any other time." I came up on the rough side of the mountain, but I was always inquisitive. I was always asking questions. I was never, ever satisfied.

JP: Did you ever marry?

Kelley: Yes.

JP: How did your husband feel about your being a bailbondsperson?

Kelley: Well, I wasn't married then. By then I had divorced him.

JP: Is he still around?

Kelley: No, he's deceased. But I'm married now again to a beautiful black man, a man that I met over thirty years ago. He was in the community struggling and so was I. It was like a chemistry when we met, but it couldn't be at that time because he was married, and I had just come out of a marriage. But when my mother passed away, which was five years ago, he called me. And he said to me, I understand your mother passed. See my mother, father, and I, we were not only just bonded by blood, we were friends. And to me that was as important as them being my parents. That just happened. No one has any control over that. But to be friends, real friends, that was beautiful. So, anyway I was in a bad state mentally and physically because with all the roads and journeys that I had taken in life, the one called death, if you lose your grip, you lose your way. And it's not easy. First my mother and then my dad. She hadn't been sick. But she had liver and pancreas cancer. You know how you never see your parents as sick or getting older, or any of those things, you know, they'll be there for you forever. I guess that was what helped me have a free spirit that I have. I was like Jonathan Livingston Seagull. I could just fly. I was free to fly. Because I knew if I fell down, Mom and Dad they were there. That's not true any longer because it's been four years now since the two of them have expired. But their legacy will live on. That's something that you always have in reach.

JP: What was your most dangerous case? First, dangerous in a sense that you had to put up a high bail and then the person jumped bail, and you had to track him or her. I don't know if that example is the same or two separate cases.

Kelley: Obviously, two separate ones. There was one man, New York as a matter of fact, and woman. They had, like what they called, a con game going. They would come to New Jersey, rent a hotel, and swindle people out of money. I would think that they are dangerous. But the real dangerous people are somebody who killed someone or drug dealers. My point of view is, that for the grace of God, go me. The fact that I didn't look down on them, the fact that I was there, not to condemn them, that's for God to do. God, in my mind, is the judge and the jury, and that's how I perceive each case. So we then had a mutual respect for each other. And I didn't have any problems out of them whatsoever.

JP: So, in addition to, like you said, by the grace of God, I guess what you kept in mind was innocent until proven guilty?

Kelley: Exactly. In the United States it's the opposite if you're black. You're guilty and then you have to prove yourself innocent. I've had some interesting cases. I had one in New York, for example, they jumped bail.

JP: How much was their bail?

Kelley: Hers was $30,000 and, you see, when a person jumps bail we have twenty days to either recover that individual or turn that promissory note into cash flow or lose your license. So I went to New York. Also, it's against a federal law to jump bail.

JP: So that's what gives bounty hunters the wherewithal to cross state lines?

Kelley: Exactly. In this case, I would always go after my own. For example, if it was a female, I would have her children's names, ages, the house that they were born in, and the school they attend. Very rarely will a mother pull her kids out of the school. If she does, she's moving to a completely different territory altogether. So once you find that child, then you find the mother.

JP: Do women jump more than males or visa versa?

Kelley: I would say, at that time, in the seventies, there weren't nearly as many women being arrested as there are today. If I bailed out five women in three months, that was a lot.

JP: To what do you attribute the increase?

Kelley: I attribute the increase to the drugs women are taking now, babies having babies, stealing to get food or clothes to take care of the bare essentials of life. And then they become good at it and start steal to sell enough of whatever just to pay rent. Or the men now, they'll put the woman on the street to prostitute themselves and to buy drugs and bring it home to them. Some of them sell their children.

JP: Sell their kids? To whom?

Kelley: Well, there are a lot of people who are not able to have children who would do anything to get a baby outside the adoption process. You see in a time and space where we've completely lost our identity to the point where it's frightening. I have mothers who knowingly let their sons go on the corner to sell drugs. And you would say, but how can a mother know this and allow it? That's because that son starts paying that phone bill, electric bill, they get good at it, they buy cars for them. We're living in some very sad times, very dangerous times.

JP: And the only place you can get a job these days is in prison?

Kelley: Yes. And that's like $40 a month. So I went to the precinct nearest to home, identified myself, I showed them my credentials. Now, had I been a man, they would take my word. I wouldn't have had to show them anything. They had me show almost my underwear proving that I was a bailbondsperson.

JP: Let's just get back to that for one minute. If you were anyone else who walked in there, they wouldn't ask for identification?

Kelley: Nothing at all. Maybe my name, but that's all. So, but for me I had to show them everything. And as a woman too. . . . But I was used to that, and I kept all my credentials prepared and what not. They said well still, what do we have to do with this? I said, "It's a federal law, sir." Federal law? I said, "Yes, bail jumping is a federal law."

JP: You mean they didn't know that?

Kelley: No. And they didn't believe me. Well, they didn't know. Even judges don't know the bail bond system, the bail bond law. So you have to take your time to educate them. So I explained to them, told them the statutes and everything that he should look up, and they had to assist me. So, the sergeant called their district attorney, and the district attorney said she's perfectly, absolutely correct. We do have to cooperate. So, they took me to this building. You know those high rises in New York? Well, that woman was on the fifteenth floor, with no elevator.

JP: Wait a minute, you knew where she was?

Kelley: Oh, yes.

JP: How did you know that?

Kelley: Well, because I had an address. She jumped bail, but she still was at that address.

JP: She went back home?

Kelley: They usually do.

JP: Why would they do that?

Kelley: Well, because they would think that the last place a person would think that they would go, be hiding at home. And that's the first place. So, I knocked on the door. First of all, the police, they were leaving me behind. You know how you run alone up the stairs, your muscles and your thighs start hurting you so bad, so they were leaving me. I had to keep going, "Oh, God, I'm going to faint." Finally, we got to the fifteenth floor. The police knocked on the door. Loud, loud knocking. And a young man opened the door. "Is your mother home?" "No, she's not here." He appeared to be thirteen or fourteen years old. We said, "Well, we have a warrant to search this apartment."

JP: Did they have one?

Kelley: Yeah. I had the warrant.

JP: You mean with a search warrant? But you don't need one. A bounty hunter doesn't need a warrant.

Kelley: Yes. Well, it depends. You see, a lot of bounty hunters work for themselves. You should have top identification. Let's say, hypothetically, you were running from the law and you had jumped bail and I was after you. See, once I recover you, let's say your bail is $10,000, that's saving the bail bonds agent $10,000. So the bounty hunter gets maybe $2,000, so the bailbondsperson or man has lost $2,000 as opposed to $10,000. But now you go on with that person's identity, certain pictures, social security number, date of birth, I mean just complete information, but you also should have a warrant. Also, they can take you across the state line, but only if their paperwork is in order. Anything other than that, they're breaking the law.

You see, you're similar to a police officer except that you're not a police officer. You do not have the power invested in you as a police officer. Although, from the bail bonds agent's point of view, what you owe is to me, you as their prisoner, as my client, because I have put up $10,000–$20,000, or whatever it is to bail you out. And what I have promised the court is that I will produce you on your due date to court, and that I will continue to produce you until a final disposition in your case has been reached, whether it be innocent, guilty, or it doesn't matter, whether you have to pay a fine, it doesn't matter, but a final disposition does have to be reached in the case. Let's say I bailed you out of jail. You didn't even return to court on your due date, and I then turned to a bounty hunter to look for you, search for you. Although, I never did it. I was my own bounty hunter. In fact, I've flown all the way to Atlanta, Georgia, for two ministers. They jumped bail on me. Oh, I couldn't believe they jumped bail. So, I flew down to Atlanta, Georgia. And I had to scream out "My name is Carolyn Kelley. I'm a bail bonds agent from the state of New Jersey" boom, boom, boom. "What, what," he said. I couldn't see him. So I pulled a chair up, stood in the chair, now I'm looking right at him. "My name is Carolyn Kelley. I'm from the State of New Jersey, bail bonds agent," showed him that all my paperwork was in order and there are two men who jumped bail on me here, and I've come to ask your assistance returning them. Of course, they can fight extradition and say I want to stay here in the state of Georgia if they want to. But that takes time and they usually lose that, and they are then extradited here, which is where the crime originated.

JP: If they fight extradition, will you lose your money?

Kelley: No. All I have to do is tell where the body is. Either the body is present or I bring a death certificate.

JP: You bring them back dead or alive?

Kelley: Yeah. So when I finished, the officer said, "We don't have anything to do with what you do up north there." I said, "But it's the law."

And he contacted his DA. Well, was his face red. It's bad enough that I'm black and a female, now I'm telling them what to do. So they said, "we know these boys. The church is down the road there. Where are you staying?" I said, "The Hyatt Regency. I'll be prepared to meet you in the lobby." I had my hat on, my gloves on down in the lobby. The police car pulled up . . .

JP: Explain why you wore hat and gloves.

Kelley: Oh, yes. I was going to church. So they drove me to the church, and we walked in the door. One was at the pulpit, and one was sitting in the front row. Well, when they saw me, they nearly died. And when the congregation realized what was happening, one lady said, ahh, lightning is going to strike her dead.

NINETEENTH-CENTURY BOUNTY HUNTERS

In the twentieth century, the profession of bounty hunting has changed very little, except that twentieth-century men and women occasionally give interviews. As in the twentieth-century era, the 1800s offered a good living to bounty hunters, particularly on the frontier. The U.S. southwest territories were lawless and wild. In addition to Native Americans, by and large those areas were white male enclaves, men in their teens and twenties. Many of them did not live to be thirty. Short of an official war, it was white on white crime at its worse. Just as in the 1990s, hand guns were the weapons of choice. Interestingly, Arizona and New Mexico harbored one or two criminal havens populated mainly by Native Americans, men of African descent, and a few women.

Most of the men (there was no evidence of female bounty hunters) were drawn to these frontiers to make money, but more often than not, they had posses or vigilantes in hot pursuit. However, so fiercely independent were the frontier townspeople, capturing a resident outlaw entailed considerable danger to the pursuers. After evaluating the risks, many pursuers decided against confronting the outlaw, and instead posted a reward for his capture—dead, alive, or headless. Enter the bounty hunter, usually alone, primarily a male of European descent. Deciding the bounty is sufficient, he mounts a hunt.

He might die trying, but try he will to capture the fugitive and turn him over to the authorities, often a U.S. deputy marshal, if the town was a territory, or an elected sheriff or town marshal in the states. Capturing the fugitive in or near the reward town was a bounty hunter's godsend. Otherwise, tracking, capturing, and transporting the prisoner would often entail a long, arduous, and very dangerous sojourn. Although precise numbers are unavailable, it is likely that significant numbers of bounty hunters died in their quest for fortune. Such a hazardous occupation bred fearless and sometimes violent, surly men who were exceptional hunters, lightning fast on the trigger, and trusting of no one.

Another downside was that a captured fugitive could be taken from the lone bounty hunter during transport, with the subsequent loss of the bounty and even his own life. Consequently, bounty hunters trained themselves to require fewer than eight hours of sleep a night or to sleep in their saddles. Tracking a fugitive for innumerable days, with minimal food, water, or baths, in every kind of weather—hot, cold, rain, sun, storms—the man's determination was boundless. As the hunter continued the quest, his horse was a most important creature, as well as a friend and savior.

Just as professional bounty hunters trusted almost no one, few people trusted the bounty hunter and most despised the surrogate lawman. In the territories, immoral and lawless behavior were the norm. Still, bounty hunters seemed to epitomize all the evil, deceit, and uncivilized actions that these lonesome pioneers hated. Hence, by choice and by force, bounty hunters were loners. Exceptions included instances when they joined gangs or hired men in their quest for a bounty. Ironically, a few bounty hunters, like Stan Rifkin and Bob Burton in the twentieth century, became as famous as the fugitives. For the most part, in the 1800s, frontier townspeople knew when strange faces arrived in their midst, and treated the bounty hunters like they had a communicable disease. Sometimes their work was particularly odious as the following true story illustrates.

True Story

In November 1875, three ranch hands turned bounty hunters shot and killed one of California's most dreaded badman, Cleovaro Chavez, at a ranch in Arizona. "On arriving at Yuma with the body, Raggio and his friends were told by the authorities that they could not collect the reward on Chavez unless they delivered the corpse to California for positive identification. Traveling with corpses was not easy in those days, so they persuaded a local doctor to sever the outlaw's head and place it in a five gallon can of alcohol. This seemed to satisfy the State of California and the three cowhands eventually collected their reward."[25]

Knowing that rejection was a near certainty, bounty hunters sought or bought friendship as well as companionship among saloon owners and its women employees; the latter, on rare occasions, were also the owners. On the other hand, the private citizen turned bounty hunter, due to lack of economic opportunities or who enjoyed the travel and pursuit of men and women, has a special place in the nation's folklore. His role in bringing law and order to the west must be recognized.[26] Vigilantes, lawful posses (there were hundreds of unlawful posses), and bounty hunters illustrated the territories' and the nation's need for government, one founded on a democratic structure, with elected, appointed, or volunteer lawmen, properly educated judges, lawyers, and average resident juries.

Those symbols of European civilization and lower economic class control were established once families and the attendant institutions, encompassing schools, churches, and banks gained permanent berths in the territories. Some men were so opposed to such institutions, they left the area, voluntarily or by force, seeking to continue a life of exploration, without women's and children's gentling influences. Those men who stayed gave up their violent lifestyle, including full-time bounty hunting presumably becoming settled and securing legal employment or entrepreneurship.

Losing the frontier equaled losing their independence, according to some men. Once the western frontier became territories, federal police arrived, along with portable courts. These law enforcement officials, actual federal representatives, were U.S. marshals who, in turn, hired deputies. There were instances when these same marshals or deputies assumed the mantle of bounty hunters, as did sheriffs and city marshals. "Many revered lawmen, principally United States Marshals; Deputy Marshals and Sheriffs were also actively involved in searching for, arresting and sometimes killing fugitives" (Traub, 299).

Apparently, these lawmen wanted more than to see justice served. They were also interested in collecting reward money in spite of the fact that the federal and various state governments often forbade them to accept it. "The possibility of getting rewards, however remote, apparently spurred lawmen to be more energetic in their pursuit of criminals. It also provided the opportunity for United States Marshals and town sheriffs to pressure those private citizens and business organizations offering a reward to increase the amount."[27]

Resisting the lure of hefty cash rewards was difficult among men who were struggling to attain middle-class status. These official lawmen—turned bounty hunter for a week or a month—were never subjected to the disparagement private bounty hunters encountered; no evidence of women peacekeepers surfaced. Conjecture is the only approach to why lawmen as bounty hunters kept townspeople's respect and admiration. Presumably, bounty hunting as a profession was despised, while occasionally pursuing a specific vicious criminal was praiseworthy.

As small businessmen, bounty hunters often worked for themselves; seeing a poster with a high reward on a wall galvanized their mounting or joining the hunt. In addition, sometimes private citizens hired the bounty hunter, and the fee was his reward. Businesses also posted rewards. "In general, these rewards were larger than the rewards offered by federal, territorial, state and city authorities. . . . The American Express Company offered a reward of two hundred dollars for the apprehension and delivery of Walter Jerome Finn who was wanted for embezzlement."[28]

One can assume there were many instances of mistaken identity and the wrong person turned over to the local sheriff, marshal, or constable, and that lives were lost as the result of high rewards. Further, vigilante justice had its heyday in the colonies as well as in the territories during the 1800s. A person was assumed guilty once captured. Significantly, vigilantes in New Mexico comprised upper and middle class people against the lower class men of European descent. Class definitions in that era are instructive. Business people and the political elite comprised the better sort; laborers, herdsmen, innkeepers, and miners, the common sort; while the proletariat involved outlaws, drifters, and any racial or ethnic minorities. As to be expected, bounty hunters were in the last category, although not listed. Bounty hunters served a vital function in this nation's early beginnings, as well as in the twentieth century. Rearresting bail jumpers, tracking law breakers with a price on their head—those mandates instilled fear in the criminals then and now. Fugitives have been known to prefer capture by local law enforcement officials than bounty hunters. After all, bounty hunters in the territories had no rules or restrictions, just a single purpose: collect the reward by any means necessary.

However, it must be acknowledged that frontier justice was little better than bounty hunter justice. "The man behind the badge practiced a highly personal capricious brand of enforcement . . . courts with inefficient judges and prosecutors, essentially incompetent, jurors unable or unwilling to apply justice."[29] Vigilantes, posse comitatus and bounty hunters behaved accordingly in this atmosphere, in the absence or breakdown of formal law.

Bounty and Crime: Frontier and Urban

As we all know, people who left their homelands for North America were motivated by the vast social and economic injustice perpetrated against them. Of course, the notable exception to this scenario is African people, who were kidnapped and held in bondage throughout the Americas. Europeans were also enslaved during our continent's early history. Plainly speaking, the majority of Anglo-Saxon Protestants were trying to escape poverty and government oppression when they arrived on these shores.

Economic growth and a burgeoning capitalistic system spawned wealth for a few, leaving an envious majority dissatisfied with their circumstances. An expanding urban population and insufficient jobs forced an exodus to the western parts of North America. Attendant throughout this upheaval were the increased and changing characteristics of crime. That specific crime control measures were needed became increasingly apparent. Still, resistance to the notion of a police force was strong. History tells us why these feelings existed, regardless of geographical area. To implement a police force that could use its legal powers and weapons against residents was a frightening idea.

The majority of Anglo-Saxon Protestants arrived as political refugees fleeing poverty, sickness, and oppression, with recent memories of government sanctioned enslavement under the auspices of serfdom. Thus, people's reluctance concerning a publicly funded police force stemmed from the immigrants' desperate attempts to avoid official abuse inherent in such European systems. Specifically, they did not want the possibility of a standing army on the horizon.

Still, crime continued rising in the cities and was unrestrained in the West. Piecemeal approaches regarding crime control emerged; offering rewards for the return of property and the criminal's arrest was an English tradition in its early law enforcement system. This became an important and accepted feature of North American law. In addition, once there was public acquiescence regarding full-time salaried police, officers devoted extraordinary energy recovering fugitives and stolen property that had a price. "Hence, the offer of a reward was the impetus for police officers to enter illegal cooperative arrangements with known thieves and fences in order to facilitate the collection of a reward."[30] As a result of such historical corruption, local police officers in the late twentieth century are barred from claiming rewards in the states on which this research focuses.

In the frontier West, lawlessness was universal. Arizona had the worst reputation, with New Mexico occupying a not-too-distant second place. The climate and environment for violence was fostered by businesspeople intent on increasing profits at any costs. Range wars, homesteading, mining, railroad, and labor interests collided repeatedly and were settled outside the legal system. This environment spawned criminal gangs as well as lone individuals eager for instant riches, regardless of who or how many people were affected or killed.

To the boiling caldron add isolation, hard drinking, gambling, limited high paying jobs, and illiteracy together with racism against black, brown, and Native people and the boiling point is reached virtually daily, that is, "lynchings, vigilante justice, gunfights . . . cowboys shooting the town."[31] Frequently, poorly paid, untrained lawmen were no match for men intent on wrongdoing; some quit in frustration, others left because of cowardice, a few joined the gangs. Still others died upholding the law and protecting their towns.

Forward-thinking people realized that business and progress would be stymied in an atmosphere of constant peril and bloodshed. Consequently, they became personally and monetarily active in law enforcement, through citizen posses, hiring private police and detective agents, as well as offering larger rewards. Bill Dunn and James Kirker are two notorious cases in point.

True Stories

Bill Dunn, "rancher, cattle rustler, law officer and bounty hunter, helped to track down criminals . . . On May 2, 1895 Bill and one of his brothers shot and killed Charley Pierce and Bitter Creek Newcomb . . . The bodies were taken to Guthrie, Oklahoma, and a five thousand dollar reward was collected . . ."[32] This is a true and very profitable example of an impressive reward and bringing back outlaws dead or alive. Jack Duncan, a Texan, killed the legendary John Wesley Hardin. Referring to Duncan as a bounty hunter, the author of this story, Rick Miller, from his book *Bounty Hunter*, said very little about Duncan's motive for pursuing Hardin.

Yet it is obvious the $4,000 reward was a perfect motivator. Duncan was a great tracker of people. Moreover, "he developed his own network of informants and sources that allowed him to keep tabs on and track down those with a price on their heads," says Rick Miller (12). Ultimately, his finest skill, continued Miller, was to "discover that information which would allow him to ferret out the quarry successfully."

Duncan began his career in law enforcement as a police officer. However, he constantly swapped his uniform for plain clothes and bounty hunting work or to go under cover. Apparently, pursuing outlaws endowed Duncan with a much higher income than did a policeman's salary. Was that not the era's (as well as currently) purpose, to garner larger profits and salaries? Critics who may complain about Duncan's success are unrealistic and unfair. In the 1990s those people would be viewed as coddling criminals and their reservations about justice denied and dismissed.

Bounty hunters and others were certainly attracted by the possibility of substantial rewards. It is argued that one outcome of private citizens taking an active role in crime was the lucrative practice of bounty hunting. As explained previously, many such men achieved legendary status, despite their "acting as judge, jury and executioner . . . [on the one hand] . . . Bounty Hunters were generally regarded as scavengers and were not popular among settlers . . . Yet, the pursuit of people was legitimated when it was engaged in by respectable law enforcement officers."[33]

The contradictory attitudes toward bounty hunters may lie in the nature of their work. Yes, for a reward they risk life and limb tracking and capturing criminals. However, people disregarded their courageous actions, labeling the reward blood money especially when collecting it for a body. Thus, some bounty hunters created a terrible impression and reputation through odious but legitimate profit-making strategies. All the same, "the reward system in the west was effective and seems to have served as a means of networking among Peaceofficers, special agents and private detectives."[34] Despite the fact that there were few full-time bounty hunters, their legacy will continue into the twenty-first century and beyond.

James Kirker comes to mind because he perfected scalping Native Americans as a business. Indeed, it is rumored that Kirker initiated scalping, and Native Americans imitated that practice. Kirker, an Irish man, was the most notorious bounty hunter. In Mexico he was known as Don Santiago Kirker. A significant number of people of European descent changed their names or added Don, giving themselves title and authority, as well as making life less troublesome for themselves as anglos in Mexico (and in the twentieth century, in Texas and New Mexico). Kirker had a price on his head when he was captured by the Apache.

Rising to be an Apache war chief, reports credit him leading raiding parties and killing people of European descent. When he tired of his Native American friends, he sought and received a pardon and fifty dollars for every scalp brought in. With a gang of bounty hunters including Native Americans, Mexicans, and European mercenaries, they took 182 scalps. Kirker's gang headed toward Chihuahua City for the reward. "Five miles from the outskirts, Kirker's rogues were met by the governor and his wife in a carriage, a brass band, and hundreds of cheering citizens waving handkerchiefs."[35]

That evening a state banquet and ball were held in their honor. "There was much excitement too because they had brought back a number of Mexican women and children who had been captives of the Apaches."[36] Obviously, the Chihuahuan townspeople accepted Kirker as a hero, but in all likelihood his bloodletting campaign sickened those far removed from the immediate situation and area. Hence, Kirker and his crew were infamous among some and heroes among others.

Different Branches of Government Providing Bounty

Bounty, or rewards, were offered for purposes other than capturing fugitives and criminals. This time government officials wanted a body, but definitely a live one. Bounties were given to men who volunteered for the Union Army in the 1860s. Actually, there was a fund: "Contributions to the bounty fund materially aided this labor," that is, military officials and politicians tried to avoid instituting a draft. Poor Europeans, mainly Irish, were against being inducted, while the wealthy and well-connected white male Anglo-Saxon usually remained at home or at the rear of battle. In Brooklyn, New York, the Board of Supervisors (of Kings County) "voted to borrow $250,000 for the purpose of paying a $300 bounty to every substitute enlisted in place of a drafted [wealthy] man."[37] Consequently, the 1863 New York City draft riots did not touch Brooklyn.

In the 1800s, the federal government offered rewards in defense of other bureaucracies, such as the Internal Revenue Service (IRS). Persons received a bounty when they provided information leading to the arrest and conviction of those impeding IRS activities or not paying taxes.

To wit, "the Postal Service Act of 2 March, 1867 appropriated $100,000 to be used by the Commissioner of Internal Revenue . . . in detecting, bringing to trial and punishing people guilty of violating internal revenue laws."[38] As the aforementioned title suggests, the post office was similarly protected regarding mail fraud. Further, Indian Affairs and the Department of the Interior were (are) among the agencies so protected with tax money rewards.

Enslavement and Bounty

Hunting and returning enslaved Africans, as well as Europeans, to the owner-kidnappers were bounty hunters' major and most profitable activities, before emancipation in accordance with the Fugitive Slave Act, first enacted in 1793[39] and strengthened in 1850.[40] Africans and Europeans escaped frequently, sometimes together. The former group was enslaved, with the latter in indentured servitude beginning in 1619 until 1865. Indeed, penalties were more severe for European runaways than Africans, especially when the fugitive had a companion of African descent. The nation's first president, George Washington, was educated by a "convict servant bought by George Washington's father."[41]

Enslaved people who escaped from their kidnappers were charged with being fugitives from labor or service, not from bondage. Newspapers carried advertisements offering rewards for their capture, preferably alive. Most rewards were in the hundreds of dollars, with a large number in the thousands. Curiously, by and large Bostonians (and Ohioans) vigorously opposed the Fugitive Slave Act of 1850, refusing to relinquish runaways. One well-respected African fugitive's plight sparked a riot when a U.S. marshal and other lawmen attempted spiriting the man out of his Boston community.[42]

Those residents hid fugitives or warned them bounty hunters were in the area. Perhaps the Bostonians' kindness stemmed from memories of similar actions taken by the English against poor Europeans like them. Kidnapping was an established activity in parts of eighteenth-century England. Poor English men and women were forced into the navy and colonial servitude. Even British children suffered kidnapping and bondage for the colonies' labor intensive industry, explains Carol Wilson (4–5).

Nevertheless, it must be acknowledged that Europeans sold themselves to get out of England's debtors' prison, notes Herrick Cheesman (20). Many people believe that European bonded servants were only English. Truth be known, the Irish and the Dutch with some French, Italian, German, and Spanish served colonial masters. Moreover, they were beaten and put in chains the same as Africans, according to comments in the *Pennsylvania Gazette*, January 28, 1728 (3).

As illuminated above, bounties were offered for the return of Europeans who tried escaping from bondage like the Africans, so noted the *Gazette*. For instance, William Williamson, absentee rice planter, keeper (kidnapper) of thirty-four enslaved men, one of whom escaped, asserted in an advertisement, "the said fellow has declared he will not be taken alive, whoever delivers his head shall be entitled to a reward of fifty pounds," *South Carolina Gazette*, July 2, 1763 (3). One could argue that bounties and bounty hunters assisted in our nation's accumulation of capital through their role in developing and maintaining burgeoning political, social, and economic structures. They were part of the shadowy underground army, establishing controls in a young nation, in league with people of wealth. Ultimately, professional bounty hunters were joined by U.S. marshals and deputies together with sheriffs and ordinary citizens in returning escaped people to bondage. The large rewards attracted a disparate group of hunters.

For instance, throughout the country, ferry boat men were numerous, and they acted as informants to both the law's opponents and supporters. It could be argued that the slave act opponents facilitated additional flights from bondage, knowing that sympathizers awaited them in the North. "The great increase in the number of fugitives after 1850 was in part due to the uneasiness felt by northern people under a legal system which made them co-conspirators with the south in a system of structured slave hunting."[43]

Of interest is that most enslaved people endured plantation life, rather than run away. "So long as a black family remained together upon one plantation, their love for one another operated as the strongest bond to prevent their departure."[44] To their credit, and understandably, Native Americans did not relinquish or return any fugitives under the law. Although native people were threatened with military retaliation and financial losses, they still maintained this policy. In cities and rural areas, patrols were organized for the purpose of keeping watch over Africans: "the security of the [free] whites is not so much dependent upon patrols as on the constant, habitual and instinctive surveillance and authority of all white people over the blacks."[45] In response to this situation, profits increased tremendously for bounty hunters during this era. But as noted, it was an extremely dangerous profession.

Quite another group provided bounty hunters and detectives with lucrative earnings. They were runaway wives who had bounties assigned to them; husbands advertised their description. Presumably most were captured and returned home. Given the dearth of women and basically no rights, it was likely difficult to remain hidden or simply disappear. Bounties and rewards occupy an important and longstanding place in North American law enforcement. Proponents argue that citizen involvement in combating crime is enhanced through this system. Opponents contend the reward structure fosters corruption among officials, especially the police, and turns residents into informants, thereby dampening neighbors' regard for one another and destroying the nation's sense of community.

CITY MARSHALS
AND CITY SHERIFFS

TWENTIETH-CENTURY CITY MARSHALS AND CITY SHERIFFS

In this section, we will examine a profession with duties that detractors say are as offensive as the bounty hunter. They maintain a low profile at all times; consequently, one seldom hears anything about them, except when an investigative journalist, crusading official, or up and coming politician sheds light on them. However, the public has specific and personal knowledge about their activities. A significant host of these pseudo law men and women earn huge rewards in any given year. The women and men are twentieth-century city marshals.

The results of this research suggested that few states have city marshals; instead constables, as well as sheriffs, are elected to execute civil judgments. New Mexico has no city marshals. A specific division in the sheriff's department handles civil matters and administers civil court. Essentially, these elected men and women and their appointed deputies carry out the same duties. Attorneys may hire private investigators as process servers and even to carry out evictions. Still, by and large, court ordered papers and dispossess notices are executed by the sheriff's department.

Arizona has three constables who perform duties that sheriffs in other states carry out. They are civil servants of the court, executing judgments, contacting debtors, and regaining rental property (through evictions). Shirley Allen, chosen Arizona's 1988 Constable of the Year, described her job: "She is responsible for serving legal documents to people involved in the court process [including] . . . ordering an abusive man to leave his home . . . carrying out court orders to seize property from people who do not pay debts."[1] Allen, age 53, worked nine and a half years as a deputy sheriff prior to her current position as constable. She explained that "her confidence on the job is boosted by her proficiency with the .38-caliber revolver she carries."[2]

Intervening in domestic problems and evicting people can turn ugly and at times may be a dangerous assignment for officers. Arizona constables serve justice court, a lower court system, executing civil papers up to $5,000. They are an integral aspect of armed law enforcement, although they wear no uniforms and travel in unmarked cars of their choice. The constables are elected from their justice precinct. A week's training is provided. They are mainly former police officers, and usually keep their training current. Hence, one week's training is sufficient. The state legislature sets fees for the services constables provide.

New Jersey's constables perform duties that have much in common with the preceding two states. Furthermore, deputy sheriffs execute judgments (and all it entails) when there are no city marshals or constables in a given town. A specific department in the sheriff's department carries out debt collection together with other process serving duties. Despite marshals' and constables' egregious work, ultimately they perform a municipal service and can increase a city's treasury by millions of dollars. They are businesspeople, and their bottom line is to increase income. New York City is a special case in which city marshals and city sheriffs work side by side, albeit oftentimes on a less than friendly basis.

New York City Marshals

The caller to a local radio talk show sounded outraged. He commented that the city marshal arrived at an apartment building for the purpose of evicting a tenant, driving a $37,000 Mercedes. Despite the caller's anger, the marshal was within the law, he or she can drive whatever suits one's fancy. In New York City, the local marshals are private entrepreneurs whose duties include evictions and impounding vehicles with traffic violations. Their profits stem from poundage and state fixed fees on evictions carried out and fees from private businesses or public agencies that hire city marshals for a flat sum to execute judgments from civil court. They do the public's (and private) dirty

Table 2.1
The Big Eight

City marshals earn flat fees for serving eviction notices, towing vehicles, and collecting civil court judgments. After giving 3.5 percent of their fees to the city, and paying staff and other operating expenses, they keep the rest. Here's what the eight highest-earning marshals earned in 1991 as they reported to the Department of Investigation:*

	Gross Income	**Net Income**
Kenneth Brand	$708,225	$481,270
Martin Bienstock	$903,727	$310,657
Linda Swift	$475,582	$287,884
Danny Weinheim	$465,822	$234,570
Ronald Moses	$241,069	$234,116
Melvin Moses	$645,253	$227,448
George Airday	$598,112	$211,695
Melvin Schwartz	$485,788	$208,122

*Compare with Table 2.2, 1977 income chart.

Source: Reprinted from an article by Serge F. Kovaleski, "Move Over, Mayor . . . Mils Are for Marshals," *New York Daily News*, 21 December 1992, 3.

work, including garnishing salaries on past-due accounts, towing parking violators' vehicles, and carrying out evictions, all the while receiving the legislated percentages.

"Move Over, Mayor . . . Mils Are for Marshals," shouted a large, bold headline in the *New York Daily News* (Kovaleski, 3). These city marshals, according to the newspaper, averaged $101,000 in 1991 with seventeen city marshals earning over $130,000, earning the same as New York City's mayor and the state's governor (see Table 2.1). Marshal Brand, their spokesman, scoffed at any suggestion that they're merchants of misery prone to overzealousness in the pursuit of deadbeats. "We are enforcing the law," said Brand in the same article. "Does anyone like enforcement officials?" Critics liken these marshals to urban bounty hunters, but note that city marshals are appointed to a five-year term by the mayor, thus affording them added legitimacy and prestige.

New York City marshals are businesspeople, yet their earnings derive from state mandated fees. As marshals in the private sector, they are hired by landlords for evictions and by attorneys or credit agencies for collections. In terms of property evictions, for example, New York City marshals are hired as collectors against those persons refusing payment after a suit is instituted and won. Garnishes and levies on bank accounts and property are instituted by marshals. These actions are carried out on a set, fee-for-service basis. Naturally, the more clients a marshal has, the bigger his/her income. For receiving, entering, and serving summonses marshals are allotted $10 for each document; executing an order of seizure against the chattel(s), $26.50; and mileage for above services, $15. These duties can yield a marshal hundreds of dollars a day and thousands a year. One marshal, Kenneth Brand, earned a million dollars in 1991.

When a marshal leaves, he or she can sell the venture to an incoming colleague, provided all the business is in the private sector. Qualifications are minimal. An application is made (a recent development), and the person receives an interview by a special committee, with additional waiting for a mayoral appointment. In the 1990s, marshals attend training classes, another new initiative. They wear (self-bought) badges, carry weapons, and most inherit their businesses from a relative. It is overt nepotism, similar to the bail bonds profession.

As explained in a 1986 description of the city marshal position, New York City can hire up to eighty-three marshals to serve as enforcement officers of the civil court. Nevertheless, they are not city employees and receive no salaries. Their earnings are the fees from creditors and landlords in connection with evictions, money collection judgments, and the seizure of property. Marshals receive 5 percent of the poundage on the latter item. Further, every city marshal having served for more than one year must pay an annual amount to New York City of $1,500. Additionally 3.5 percent of the gross fees, including poundage received during the preceding year, must also be paid to the city.

Although marshals are a state legislative creation and supervised by the city's Department of Investigation with the judicial appellate division promulgating rules and regulations, marshals are appointed by the mayor with the recommendation of a fifteen-member marshals committee. Six are selected by the mayor and the presiding justices of first and second judicial departments, with the remaining three committee members chosen by New York City law school deans. The latter members have a one-year term while the former serve terms concurrent with the mayor's.[3] An applicant's qualifications for a marshal's position involve residing in the city of New York and a joint $20,000 bond (marshal and surety) ensuring shared liability regarding any complaints about the marshal during the execution of his or her duties. Concerning education, since 1983 applicants must have a high school diploma or an equivalent and must have completed a two-week training program. A prior two years or more service as marshal satisfies the high school diploma requirement. No marshal can have outside employment or participate in either a trade or business that could create an actual or potential conflict of interest.[4]

In the end, it is important to make clear that "pursuant to article 16 of the New York City Civil Court Act, Marshals became officers of the

Table 2.2
Net Incomes Derived from Fees and Poundage of City Marshals, 1977

Fees & Poundage Gross Income Category	Fees & Poundage Average Gross Income	Number of Marshals	Average Net Income
Under $24,999	$12,640	5	Not Available
25,000–49,999	$38,921	10	$16,366
50,000–74,999	$69,619	7	$28,491
75,000–99,999	$86,680	9	$32,878
100,000–149,999	$123,736	8	$55,543
150,000–199,999	$175,189	12	$68,893
Over 200,000	$276,280	11	$80,628

Source: New York City Department of Investigation.

civil court of New York City."[5] Hence marshals wear two hats, and opponents contend that the primary hat is profits, with service a distant second. All the same, their supporters maintain that debt collection and evictions are better performed by marshals because reinstatement of debtors' prison, outlawed in England 1869, is the alternative. On a positive slant, marshals stand between economically distressed consumers and prison. Granted, one's property may be confiscated, but one still has her or his freedom. New York City marshals' services, like their Arizona and New Jersey constabulary colleagues, are bittersweet and unique.

Let us review the details about poundage (see Table 2.2). City marshals receive poundage fees when an eviction is effectuated. That is, the fee, $37.50 per room in 1995, is premised on how many rooms of furniture he/she removes and places in storage. Also, there are storage charges. Marshals and their relatives are prohibited from owning anything that may conflict with their mandated responsibilities (e.g., storage centers, towing companies, car pounds). Even so, opponents allege that marshals do have business connections in those enterprises. Further, according to detractors, city oversight of marshals is minimal, especially given New York City's dire economic situation. Funding for inspectors and investigators do not have high priority in the city's budget.

Consequently, opponents suspect the worse case scenario may be true. Using anecdotal information, city marshals may be violating or stretching the laws and regulations governing them with impunity. Who would be the wiser? At minimum, victims may suffer property loss as a result of unchecked infractions by the city marshals. From previous remarks we can deduce that New York City marshals are cognizant of

Table 2.3
Allegations Concerning City Marshals, 1974–1977*

		1974	1975	1976	1977
a)	Landlord & Tenant Matters				
	1. Missing Property	92	89	70	78
	2. Damaged Property	0	5	5	6
	3. No 72-hour Notice	19	32	33	25
	4. Other	26	25	32	25
	Subtotal	137	151	140	134
b)	Collection of Judgment				
	1. Failure to collect	32	34	35	65
	2. Improper service of the execution	24	26	13	5
	3. Overcollecting	9	18	9	20
	Subtotal	65	78	57	90
c)	Overcharging of fees	16	17	15	6
d)	Recovery of chattel	3	9	5	8
e)	Failure to comply with the law or directives of the Department of Investigation	41	32	52	54
	Total	262	287	269	292

*The Marshals Handbook, July 1986, reveals that the Marshals Bureau "annually receives thousands of complaints."

Source: Reprinted from the Legislative Office of Budget Review, New York City Sheriffs, New York City Marshals, A Comparative Study. Report to the Committee on the Legislative Office of Budget Review of the New York City Council, December 28, 1978.

the animosity they generate. The marshals' assignments usually eliminate them from winning a popularity contest.

That is, certain features of the city marshalcy's operation figure prominently when he/she performs normal duties, such as vehicles being seized when the owner is on her/his way to work and evictions, particularly during the holidays. The debtor, believing he/she is a victim of enthusiastic judgment executions and feeling so aggrieved, may file complaints describing misconduct and unlawful behavior[6] (see Table 2.3). Critics believe such charges are the iceberg's tip and that the majority of people in a financial quandary, especially the very low income, refrain from reporting abuses and violations of their rights.

Often the most pressing concerns among the working class are meeting life's basic needs. Still, once an individual, as well as a family, has accepted their plight and resettled and has taken inventory of their meager assets, the shame as well as mental anguish associated with the marshal's actions begin emerging, and a small number will, eventually, file a complaint describing what occurred. According to the table, landlord-tenant disputes, missing property, and the city marshal's failure to comply with the law received the most allegations concerning wrongdoings.

Be mindful that missing property is a serious issue because financially strapped people can barely afford food, shelter, and clothing, let alone replace a television set, stereo system, iron, or bed, for example. More painful is the awful realization that they might never have sufficient funds to replace their household goods. This revelation and loss of basic items owned by most North Americans disables economically disadvantaged people, leaving them further outside the nation's mainstream. Another point that must be raised is the notion that New York City marshals work hard at filling the city's coffers, as opposed to city sheriffs' so-called lackadaisical approach.

One marshal commented that sheriffs only work nine to five, while marshals devote ten to twelve hours a day to their job. Without a major effort, the former would not make a decent living for his/her family. City sheriffs, on the other hand, who also have towing responsibilities, cost the city money because they are civil servants receiving little benefits, among them health and pension, to paraphrase a city report criticizing sheriffs and marshals. The marshal's admonition received an unprecedented reaction from the sheriffs' department and nearly caused the city marshals' vocation's demise. Admittedly, much of the faultfinding about sheriffs had some truth as its basis. A full explanation is provided in the city sheriffs' section.

At this point we will examine the most serious negative features attributed to the city marshalcy. New York City marshals have an allegiance to creditors who hire them and thus cannot be impartial, as the law requires. There are charges of not delivering court papers and notices resulting in default judgments against the poor, criminal activity including bribery, overcharging, kickbacks, stealing property, political payoffs, delegating work only a city marshal (as an officer of the court) must perform, lying about scheduled evictions, and the list continues.[7] These accusations, along with the notion of tremendous sums gotten at someone else's expense, have given New York City marshals a bad reputation. Let us determine whether the sheriffs are more reputable.

New York City Sheriffs

The New York City sheriff's department, in the 1960s–1970s performed in a less than stellar manner. New York City's Budget Review and Comparative Study, in 1978, on sheriffs and marshals, considered the possible ramifications of a mayoral proposal that called for eliminating city marshals,[8] giving sheriffs the marshals' workload. However, the measure failed. Fourteen years later, the mayor (David Dinkins, at the time) decided to expand the office of sheriff "to serve as the city's central collection agency to whittle away at the four billion dollars in unpaid fines, fees and other accounts receivable due to the city" accumulated over years (Dinkins). Not surprisingly, ultimately that too failed. A press release from Mayor Dinkins' office, July 12, 1990, elevated the city sheriff's position to an administrative and management job, allowing for more flexible supervision. It sometimes takes a century to bring about change, as the subsequent facts illustrate.

New York City was encouraged to disband the sheriff's jury since their activities wasted taxpayers money. Its "function is to decide mental competency cases involving at least $500,000" (Goldstein, 78). A nine-member state investigation commission urged the legislature to abolish Manhattan's sheriff's jury. According to the *New York Times*, December 12, 1976, "The Sheriff's Jury . . . is divided into three panels, each of which wines, dines and bestows expensive gifts on top-level public officials and judges at an annual banquet . . . [they] even have a rehearsal dinner . . . on such occasions, certain members volunteer to test proposed menus. An even more select group of invitees attend and an even more costly array of gifts is bestowed" (Goldstein, 78). This institution was established in colonial days. Then, as in the 1970s, its members are the most distinguished and influential people in the business community. This was the second time opponents have questioned its importance and lobbied for the jury's demise, wrote Tom Goldstein in the *New York Times* article. They lost that particular campaign, which was another illustration of tradition winning the battle of changes.

Reporter Warren Moscow waxed nostalgic about New York city sheriffs (exempting deputies) of old, when former Mayor Dinkins, on July 12, 1990,[9] made them mayoral appointees, abandoning the civil servant status they held for forty-eight years. An aside during the 1940s, officials in Cleveland were much impressed by New York reinstating sheriffs and staff to classified civil service, with all positions filled from competitive examination lists.

To further explain, in January 1942, New York voters achieved this feat by using the ballot through a charter amendment. They accomplished reform under the effective argument that these five county offices were spoils-ridden, wasteful, inefficient, and even corrupt. Despite a lawsuit, which was sustained by the appeals court, the initiative served as a model in other cities seeking ways to advance agency effectiveness while reducing costs. Indeed, in the first fifteen months,

New York City's "new Sheriff made an actual savings of $404,580.53, which represents a savings of approximately $300,000 per year," as noted in *Greater Cleveland: A Bulletin on Public Business.*

Back to Moscow's comments, downsizing staff, 1990s language for layoffs, was a basic component of decisive savings. He noted that earlier shrievalty responsibilities were virtually identical to the 1990s. However, sheriffs were nominated and elected by the dominant political party. Mayor Fiorello LaGuardia characterized the deputies as clubhouse loafers, wrote Moscow. Sheriffs toiled for the political machine as district captains, and some were suspected of accepting bribes. Tom Farley was notorious and went down in New York City's history with the nickname of "Tin Box Tom." Farley claimed all his wealth came from a tin box at home. Sheriffs operated under a fee system, like New York City marshals, earning $100,000 a year in some instances. That era, commented Moscow, the mayor and governor's salaries were $10,000.

Although present day critics maintain that city marshals are far too powerful and should be reined in, they also note that the sheriff's office operates under an annual deficit, and also note its staff lack substantive administrative and managerial skills. Civil service staff and deputies perform clerical tasks at great costs to New York City. On the other hand, "the Marshals have over five times as many support staff per enforcement officer . . . and more advanced office equipment, as noted in the study" Legislative Office of Budget Review, *New York City Sheriffs, New York City Marshals: A Comparative Study* (10).

Nonetheless, these support services could and should have been assumed by non-law clerical employees, freeing more deputies to work in the field, thereby increasing the agency's productivity and cost effectiveness. Additionally, sheriffs' and marshals' responsibilities overlap in many areas, serving judicial processes, executing court mandates together with apprehending traffic violators or impounding their vehicles. Marshals have essentially the same duties, although private judgment creditors' work entails a great deal of their time. Basically, the aforementioned professional creditors employed city sheriffs only when the law requires. Ultimately, this redundancy caused competition and some mutual hostility.

A new city sheriff, Philip Crimaldi, fostered surprise and concern among marshals and the public. Sheriff Crimaldi was determined that the agency would earn its keep by increasing the city's coffers. Credit card machines were installed in deputy sheriffs' cars, thus enabling motorists to pay outstanding tickets and keep their vehicles from being impounded immediately. Sensitivity training was formalized, and he outfitted the approximately one hundred four deputies in new uniforms "to help motorists identify them," said reporter Rita Delfiner (23).

His efforts paid off. "The Sheriff recovered $35 million and all of it went to the city. But the program cost the city $4 million. Hence the [City] Sheriff returned almost nine dollars for every one dollar the city invested. Marshals returned almost seven dollars for every one dollar they kept," wrote Serge F. Kovaleski in "More for This Town's Sheriff?" Crimaldi noted, "If Marshals get sick . . . they cannot tow because by law the Marshals must be present." City Marshal Alfred Locascio observed in the same article, "There is plenty of room for co-existence."

No truer words were spoken. The combined monies turned over to the city were $51 million, minus what the city spent and the marshals' profits. Despite those efforts, this was a proverbial drop in the bucket because of the "$4 billion in unpaid fines, fees and other accounts receivable due to the city," according to the *Chief Leader* ("Dinkins Signs Bill," July 20, 1990, 1). Moreover, the announcement that Mayor Dinkins signed a bill providing appointive status for city sheriff and expanding the sheriffs' office into the "city's central collection agency" was reprinted. Since 1943 the city sheriffs' position was secured through competitive civil service examinations.

Although Dinkins has turned back the clock, sheriff's deputies remain civil servants. Moscow observed, "had [the mayor] tried to do the same for deputies, the outcry would have been loud and long" (4). Foreboding changes continued in 1996. That is, the city sheriff's supervising agency is New York City's Department of Investigation. No longer does the sheriff have direct mayoral access. He and his staff may wonder whether the office is on its way out.

New York City's sheriff department was in the limelight for a while due in part to former Sheriff Crimaldi's aggressive tactics in debt collection, unpaid parking tickets specifically. One motorist alleged being beaten when he photographed deputies impounding a car. Under charges later dropped, the motorist was arrested. He has filed a $20 million lawsuit, naming the city and Sheriff Crimaldi as defendants. The latter has been criticized for his department's strong arm approach of law violators. Proponents are delighted that sheriff's deputies have recovered more than $70 million in unpaid tickets and other fines over the past two years, thus rivaling New York City marshals in debt collection. The once sleepy sheriff's office has awakened and become a tiger. Still, critics point out that "the twenty outstanding claims filed against his [Crimaldi's] office are a substantial amount."[10] A few critics labeled him a cowboy sheriff, inferring that Crimaldi's office had frontier connotations. Notwithstanding, it is obvious that debt collection can be a profitable business, either private or public, especially when economic displacement occurs. Also, even mild financial slowdowns can wreck havoc, thus triggering loan defaults.

Corporations have a role in the dead-beat-debtor syndrome. Their reluctance to pay what is owed stems from the confidence of sheer size and political access. In an April 15, 1992, *New York Newsday* interview with Sheriff Crimaldi, he stated that other agencies and businesses besides the Parking Violations Bureau, from which city sheriffs collected, had outstanding debts (93). "There are four main judgment debtor agencies. The largest one is Parking, with an outstanding debt of $1.2 billion. Next is the Finance Department, regarding nonpayment of taxes . . . this [uncollected revenue] ranges from $400 million to $700 million . . . followed by environmental whose auspices encompass fire, buildings and sanitation and $300 million due them not including the Taxi and Limousine Commission, which owes something in excess of $50 million."

But here again the city's corporate entities, such as the food merchants, are major wrongdoers. They owe a $100 million judgment debt, commented Crimaldi. Why these debts go unpaid, according to Crimaldi, is because the city has a paper tiger image—and reality. Crimaldi's aggressiveness earned him media labels of bounty hunter and cowboy. Moreover, Crimaldi stepped on powerful people's toes and challenged the reasons marshals reaped millions of dollars, "while the [City] Sheriffs' office lost three-quarters of a million dollars a year" (*New York Newsday*, April 15, 1992, 93).

Crimaldi, in the same *Newsday* interview, commented that it was curious that "all the brains that have operated this city for years allowed the Sheriffs to lose money while Marshals and private collection agencies were allowed to earn millions of dollars doing what the Sheriff was empowered to do." At any rate, such unusual straightforwardness, especially by a bureaucrat, likely advanced his subsequent departure in 1995.

Contrast Crimaldi's flamboyance and controversy with the laid-back, consummate professional approach of the current city sheriff, Raul Russi. He is the first sheriff of Spanish-speaking heritage. Appointed by the mayor, the position is (in 1996) consolidated under the Finance Department, with the deputy finance commissioner supervising the city sheriff. Despite this monumental change, eliminating direct mayoral access and control, Sheriff Russi is enthusiastic about the agency's role and welcomes all challenges. Russi believes effective law enforcement in New York City, particularly judgment collection, requires increased centralization.

A case in point, the U.S. system has prompted greater police cooperation together with more logical division of duties, notes Russi. Be that as it may, whether city marshals will merge under the city sheriff's supervision or face elimination is a fascinating question. The twentieth century has as many well-known sheriffs and deputies, as in colonial days. Two were discussed earlier, but G. Gordon Liddy probably has the most name recognition of any present day law enforcement officer. Deputy Sheriff Liddy, overseer of Nixon's Watergate scandal, gained early fame in the 1960s by arresting Timothy Leary, the psychedelic expert, during a house raid in Millford, New York (*New York Times*, June 1, 1996, 12). Deputy sheriffs are, behaviorally, certainly akin to their supervisors, in terms of their own infamous members. Certainly, to paraphrase City Marshal Brand, there is enough city judgment collection work for everyone—over a billion dollars, observes former City Sheriff Crimaldi. Theirs are venerable and remunerative occupations. City marshals' and sheriffs' histories offer us an intriguing glimpse of debt collection's procedures.

True Story

According to a 1992 article in *New York Newsday*, overtones of the Arizona sex discrimination case (see "Ex-Deputy Called 'Gal' Settles for $405,000," *Star Globe Arizona*, December 15, 1983, 1) surfaced when a Hispanic female deputy sheriff joined New York City's sheriffs department (Arce, 36). The department staff was comprised of 97 percent white women and males. Subsequently, those numbers changed to 55 percent people of color under Sheriff Crimaldi. However, just three Hispanic women were deputies, out of one hundred forty. Said Crimaldi to the concerned deputy, "This is not a job many women apply for." "It seems his recruitment campaign didn't include women, Hispanic or otherwise," commented reporter Rose Marie Arce (36). "He can't let his drive for more effective law enforcement get lost in the muddle of race and gender politics," continued Arce.

Crimaldi supporters focused proudly on the fact that under his stewardship more fees have been collected than in the past fifty years (Arce, 36). Crimaldi should be commended for his economic efforts and dedicated service to New York City. But he must be aware and acknowledge that women need well paying employment, just like men. A significant number are heading families and have a major cost that men seldom encounter, specifically child-care. Gender considerations should be made, given that women are also taxpayers.

Interviews with City Marshals

Edited Excerpts of Interview. New York City Marshal Z (Anonymous)

Born in 1909, Z was ambitious and a trail blazer; being a marshal was her primary dream. Z took a job in a marshal's office, knowing that when some marshals left or died, their wives could be appointed in their husband's place. But in 1961 the Marshal for whom Z worked died, and Z was appointed city marshal and continued the business. The business of the office was processing and carrying out evictions for the New York City Housing Authority. Z was the first marshal in the family, and they were unimpressed, even fearful about the new occupation. Z ignored the family's comments and negative remarks, but almost quit after the first assignment. "After my first eviction, I cried like a baby." It was a terrible thing to do to anyone, Z explained.

As the years passed, Z adjusted to the profession's responsibilities, realizing one was just carrying out the courts' orders. Still, during every eviction Z felt overcome with sadness and pity.

Indeed, Z was scolded several times by superiors for attempting to help a desperate family. That is, she might delay the eviction while the family contacted New York City Housing Authority officials, or Z might advise the family about their rights in an eviction proceeding. Z, as noted, was admonished and warned against playing a social worker's role. "Just mind your business and follow orders," Z was told.

Thirty-three years later, Z still worries about the people to whom eviction is a terrible reality, although currently Z hires others for the actual procedure. Z confided to me about the personal acquaintances Z has with many of the families-in-crisis. She will continue risking censure by warning them of impending legal actions, urging that the family contact authorities regarding payment—either New York City housing or social service officials. The latter officials are often the culprit in this eviction proceeding, according to Z.

As a result, a call or visit by the client or social services regarding the problem usually forestalls an eviction, provided that a corresponding notification from social services to the housing authority assures that payment will arrive shortly. (In the 1990s social services are automatically informed of an imminent eviction.) Z notes, happily, that less than a hundred evictions a year from New York City Housing are carried out. In 1993, there were ninety; 1992—seventy-four; 1991—seventy-two; 1990—seventy-three evictions. By contrast, New York City marshals working in the private sector for landlords average fifteen a day.

When asked what City Marshal Z does on a given day, "I am a paper pusher" was the answer. In response to a request for details, Z explained there are numerous steps in the eviction process. Specifically, the New York City Housing Authority officials send a list requesting warrants; from that list appropriate forms are completed and forwarded to civil court by Z. Ten to twenty days later, warrants and seventy-two hour notices to vacate premises arrive at Z's office. The New York City Housing Authority is notified in writing that warrants are in hand. Z asks formally whether the authority wants the seventy-two hour notice served. With the authority's permission, a process server hands the seventy-two hour notice to the tenant if possible.

In addition, a copy of the seventy-two hour document is sent by certified return-receipt mail. Finally, a copy is glued on a tenant's door. Tenants can and usually do get a stay of the eviction and vacate the premises or pay the required rent before actual eviction takes place. Should a tenant be forced to leave, professional movers and the police handle the case. No one is evicted on Sundays.

Z confided that the funniest case occurred many years ago upon arriving with the police to carry out an eviction. A naked person opened the door, and Z was shocked and ran back downstairs, to the laughter of police and the tenant.

The most frightening occurrence entailed the police entering an apartment through a window because the tenant did not open the door when ordered. Once the police gained entry, it was determined the person was dead. At no time has a tenant attempted bodily harm against Z. However, Z has received "many tongue lashings." Z explains that their frustration, rage, and fright are understandable, and ignores their comments. "I can easily put myself in the tenant's place; nobody wants to be in the street," Z said many times during the interview.

Essentially, a marshal's job is not dangerous. However, as explained previously, Z's family, at the beginning of the career, worried about Z's safety, urging that she switch to another occupation. Z refused their advice because she likes the job. When explaining marshal's duties in general, Z noted that most times danger is not an issue for males or even females. Marshals are specialists, that is, they receive assigned jobs, like Z, in the public arena, or they can take over someone's private practice upon becoming a city marshal.

Excerpts from Telephone Interview: Ken Kelly—Director,
Governmental Affairs New York City Marshals Association, Edited

There are fifty marshals. By law there can be no more than eighty-three city marshals. There is a five-year term appointment by the mayor. Marshals must live in New York City during their entire term. Marshals are regulated by the Department of Investigation (DOI). Actually it is the Department of Internal Affairs for the entire city. All city agencies have an inspector general at DOI; within DOI is the Marshals' Bureau. Its supervisor is the Commissioner of Investigation.

Marshals can enforce Supreme and civil court judgments. Previously, marshals handled judgments up to $25,000, but that has just increased to $50,000 or less. To date, the amount is $100,000. Their power and responsibilities include: city parking violations, seizing judgment debtor's cars, and garnishing salaries. Additionally, they do landlord/tenant work for the city, specifically taking possession of an apartment. Evictions for private entities are carried out also. Among the accounts New York City marshals have are with Con Edison and Brooklyn Union Gas, and in addition, New York City marshals can take the meters from individuals and businesses for nonpayment. Legal authority is theirs to break into and secure the premises if Con Edison, for instance, approves. A Marshal must be present as an officer of the court [for all official activities].

At small claims court, the marshal can go after the person or private entity, but they are officers of the court. Other cities use the sheriff's department for the duties just described. New York City is so big that marshals are needed. They receive poundage fees and 5 percent of judgments. When two cars are impounded, marshals get a $45 fee and 5 percent of judgment poundage. The *Daily News* article discussed poundage fees that apply to judgments. In addition, marshals' fees are incurred when executing judgment. They receive $45. All fees are statutory. New York City marshals are not peace officers. They are not required to carry a firearm, but with a permit usually do so. Their arrests are a citizen's arrest, and when "a situation" happens, police are requested. Most of the time housing police are called to the scene during a public housing eviction.

Most marshals work a minimum of twelve hours a day. Their salaries' have a wide range. Those making six figures are struggling to do so. Marshals are appointed, and since there is no fixed salary, she or he must find work. When marshals are first appointed they get on a waiting list for work; some eight or nine of them are currently on the list so they must develop other business. A marshal may work for any private sector person or business, for example, American Express. The latter will definitely go to a marshal rather than sheriff. Entrepreneurs know that sheriffs are civil servants and believe they will not work as hard or maintain long hours. Sheriffs work 9 A.M. to 5 P.M. and can finish an assignment tomorrow because they are on the city payroll. Marshals will make money and complete the job. City marshals are not indemnified by the city. Any lawsuits are borne by the marshals. Often the city uses marshals rather than sheriffs. Employing the former entails no salaries or benefits or possible lawsuit expenses. Also, marshals have successfully lobbied [1997] and won the right to enforce civil judgments in the Supreme as well as Family Courts.

All marshal applications are handled by the Department of Investigation. This mayoral appointment is akin to a judgeship, and there is ample opportunity to make money. Most marshals take five years to build their business. There are no specific qualifications other than living in the city. However, there is currently a background check, instituted a few years ago, by New York City's Department of Investigation. At present there are thirty marshal positions available; some have retired or died. There is a need for more marshals because they cannot do all the work.

Critics argue that marshals should not be in law enforcement because the city should not use police officers as bill collectors or evictors. [On the other hand] marshals can be in the judicial process, but not perform any of the uniform personnel's services. Permitting marshals to carry a badge and have one firearm are fine, with a license. Their work can be risky.

Marshals have offices to maintain and staff. Officially, there are no geographic boundaries for private business. However, city work may be assigned to a marshal with special boundaries. All marshals do both city and private work. But some marshals do mostly city work. The City Housing Authority may select eight or nine marshals to do work for them. Selections are made according to seniority. It is unlikely these marshals will get civil service status, despite working closely with the city, because marshals have business status, a recognition that they are entrepreneurs.

City marshals work closely and cooperate with city and state government towing agencies, including the New York State Police. Characteristically, New York City marshals are concerned about any legislative action that impacts their livelihood. Thus, marshals have a liaison person with various agencies as well as a marshals' lobbyist, paid with marshal's membership dues. The current president of their organization, Alfred LoCascio, has been in office twenty years.

Marshals can place a levy on a business, that is, a notice that refusal to pay judgment will result in the seizing of assets. Papers are given along with an in-person, two-week warning and six letters by mail, before a judgment is executed by the marshal. Can people negotiate with marshals when a judgment is about to be executed? Yes, with Con Edison or private entities, but not for city work. For example, if a bill is $1,000 and a person has $500, Con Edison can instruct marshals to accept what is offered.

Still other businesses may want the total amount owed. All in all it is a frustrating and depressing job. Many people can't pay their bills. Meters are removed or abandoned. Squatters or unemployed people steal electricity or gas. Today, in the 1990s, meters are removed from nice, middle class homes. People are struggling to survive. Moreover, they need their cars to go to work, yet marshals will tow them. It is their job.

NINETEENTH-CENTURY CITY MARSHALS AND CITY SHERIFFS

The tradition of marshalcy began in England as a judicial service and crossed the Atlantic Ocean. Marshals served the original colonies: Jamestown, Plymouth, and Massachusetts Bay. They supported the courts and cared for prisoners until the seventeenth century ended. A few colonies, like Massachusetts Bay, eliminated the marshalcy, substituting the office of sheriff, while Georgia continued using town marshals until the American Revolution (Ball, *United States Marshals*, 243). Those marshals had relatively safe positions compared with their frontier colleagues, as we shall soon discover.

Pat Garrett was one of New Mexico's most famous town marshals, as well as sheriff. Those titles were interchangeable in that era. Having to police large New Mexican and Arizonan territories while receiving low wages fostered the practice of a law officer holding more than one position. "Constables were Deputy Sheriffs; Sheriffs were Deputy Federal Marshals. The tradition of cross deputization often went to extremes and could produce conflicts of interest," according to Larry Ball ("Frontier Sheriffs at Work," 283). Like most working people, earning a good living was a major issue among lawmen.

For instance, frontier jails were veritable money-making gold mines, although deplorable inmate conditions existed. Some city marshals were even paid by the number of prisoners. Naturally more arrests were made. Others made lucrative arrangements with businesses for prison labor. (A return to this practice is occurring in many states in the 1990s.) Moreover, these law enforcement officers increased their income by offering personal services to prisoners, even allowing escapes, explains Frank Prassel in *The Western Peace Officer* (93).

Prassel further states "some Town Marshals were selected according to their association with and support of local vice interests. Officers with such connections quite naturally tended toward open corruption and debauchery."[11] Regardless of that economic and sordid aspect of law enforcement, the majority of frontier peace officers spent their lives facing down and capturing desperate men and women who were trying to line their coffers, albeit illegally.

In any case, Garrett exemplified the myths and stories of western lawmen in the 1800s. Quick on the draw, saving the local populace from outlaws' murderous behavior and rowdy cowboys, Pat Garrett stood head and shoulders among famous lawmen. To wit, his reputation stemmed from having slain the New York City–born Billy the Kid. The marshal sheriff, a distinguished hunter of desperadoes, was in turn killed by outlaw Wayne Brazil on February 29, 1908, near Las Cruces, New Mexico. Turning himself in, Brazil claimed self defense, although it was proved that Pat Garrett was shot in the back of the head.[12] The shooter was charged with murder.

True Story

City Marshal Joe Carson in Las Vegas, New Mexico, joined the list of fearless lawmen when he faced four horse thieves on a cold January night in 1880. A gunfight erupted, and over forty shots were fired. The marshal was hit nine times and died. The outlaws were wounded, and one was jailed still bleeding. Subsequently, the two escapees were captured and, along with the jailed murderer, hanged by vigilantes. The gunmen and their leader were in their early twenties; two were just twenty-one. Western justice was often swift, without any benefit of lawyers or courts. Although frontier peace officers' bravery in upholding the law are unquestioned, there are several instances when marshals were on the wrong side of justice.

Milt Yarberry is an excellent example of law enforcement's vicious aspects. He was the first town marshal in Albuquerque,[13] despite being a rogue and using an assumed name. Yarberry, who had been unceremoniously ousted from Caron City, Colorado, for managing a dishonest saloon, mortally wounded his first victim on March 27, 1881.[14] Claiming self defense, although the deceased was unarmed, townspeople decided it was the victim's fault, and the marshal escaped prosecution. Yarberry shot the second man a few months later, repeating his self defense plea. But this time townspeople were unconvinced. In February 1883, Yarberry received the death penalty, becoming the first town marshal so charged. For the execution, "Scores of citizens had been sent engraved invitations to the hanging, and others not so favored, paid as much as a dollar for standing room on nearby rooftops . . . an almost carnival-like atmosphere prevailed."[15] Milt Yarberry was the first and last execution of a peace officer in the New Mexico territory.[16] Life was cheap and temporary, lawman or not. So here we see two completely disparate lawmen, Yet both symbolized, in their own special way, the life and death conditions inherent in our nation's western areas.

Despite these killings having taken place in New Mexico, some historians argue that Arizona's sordid nature surpassed all western towns and territories. Illustrating this issue perfectly is Evans Coleman's essay written in the early 1900s. Coleman writes that he met Charley Caneer, a member of the Clanton Gang, one of the most deadly, notorious group of men to terrorize frontier regions.

The gang member said, "Of all the places I have ever been, Apache County was the worst—was the best rendezvous for outlaws. . . . In all my association with bad men, I had never seen as bad a collection as was in Apache County," noted Coleman.[17] Even a few women joined the ranks of criminals. Arizona had a female robber named Pearl Hart. She was "the last of the lady road agents."[18] Before turning to robbing stages, she mugged men after luring them to her room. In 1899, Hart was captured, sentenced to five years, and released in 1902.[19]

Any history of city marshals is incomplete unless Virgil Earp and his deputized brothers are given their due. Wyatt Earp, the most famous brother, participated in, and perhaps instigated, the celebrated gunfight at O.K. Corral, October 26, 1881. So much controversy surrounds this shoot-out that separating fact from myth is extremely difficult, but we do know the Earp brothers and Doc Holliday were accused of murder. According to the *Historical Atlas of the Outlaw West*, Wyatt and Holliday were jailed for a time, but the shooting was subsequently deemed justified by the local magistrate (Patterson, 5). Having turned away from law enforcement, Virgil Earp and his wife left Tombstone the following year, two days after Morgan Earp was killed. Wyatt and Doc Holliday stayed behind. There are other less well-known stories about lawful and unlawful frontier peace officers. Their numerous adventures are equally interesting; however, space does not permit a thorough depiction of their lives.

It is apparent that frontier marshals' responsibilities differed greatly from New York City marshals, as well as among the constables in New Jersey and New Mexico. The first New York City marshals were appointed by the mayor in 1655. Essentially, their duties were the same as twentieth century counterparts, with some differences. Indeed City Marshal Dirck Van Schelluyne, appointed January 8, 1655, had duties described as "charged to distrain by executing judgments on delinquent city debtors . . . a fee of four gilders wampum, and Constables were paid for watching on New Year's eve."[20] Also, they were jail keepers, small-pox guards, and marshals of the militia.

Constables' duties typically paralleled the marshal's and in many instances were duplicative. Lodowyck Pos was appointed by the city and county to collect fines. "The mayor's court, orders that the City Marshal's fee be paid for out of the money of a special court."[21] The preceding declaration was recorded after the new marshal's appointment on January 25, 1670.[22] Thus, history tells us that New York City marshals have been in service for centuries. Even in colonial times, the government and its residents had a need for city marshals to collect debts. Average business people were either leery or uncomfortable tracking and challenging debtors.

One may assume, as long as there are businesses, there will be deadbeats. Consequently, somebody has to fill the unpopular position of debt collector. Present day New York City marshals, along with constables in the other two states, have taken on the challenge. Their jobs pay well, considering the minimum education requirements and, in the twentieth century, the addition of pensions (New York City). Debt collectors by whatever name (sheriff, constable, marshal) will likely be with us for many more years; after all, they have been engaged in the profession, essentially, since this nation's industrial birth.

The first New York City sheriff was appointed by the governor in 1665. Colonial duties encompassed seizing debtors' property, building dunking stools, summoning twelve men to discuss and rule on major issues, such as arranging for a jail on the upper floors of city hall and determining the acreage needed for a new street. In addition, city sheriffs constructed gallows, administrated and maintained city jails and prisoners, repaired jails, took the census, secured vagabonds, and conducted sheriff sales.

As New York City expanded, each borough had a city sheriff until 1941 (Stokes and Dodd, 272). The preceding year had added significance because all (five) county sheriff offices in New York City were abolished. Their functions and powers were transferred to city sheriffs, except for the transport of criminal prisoners (*Guide*, 317). The city sheriff and deputies were responsible for all civil prisoners. Hence, as in the 1990s, the city sheriffs' powers extended to executing all court mandates, except when imposed by law, on the police or corrections departments.

Edited Telephone Interview: New York City Marshal (Anonymous)

JP: How long have you been a Marshal?

A: Oh, about fourteen years.

JP: How did you get into this line of work?

A: Through the normal application procedures, the Department of investigation.

JP: Why did you decide to go into this profession?

A: After having twenty-one years in another field and getting close to retirement, I decided I wanted to do something significantly different. With that in mind, a friend of mine, who was at that point a marshal, explored with me the possibilities and piqued my interest, and so I pursued it.

JP: That previous field, was it related to law enforcement?

A: Not at all. I was in higher education.

JP: Tell me what you do on an average day?

A: Primarily, the responsibilities of a marshal is to enforce the orders and execute warrants from the civil court. Mainly landlord/tenant work is my area of concentration. I do work with the utilities like Con Edison, and I do income and property executions.

JP: And how do you carry out your duties?

A: With the warrants from the courts, which is signed by a judge, issued by the court, we're empowered to take legal possession of apartments from tenants who are delinquent in their rent payments, or tenants who for one reason or another has a warrant issued against them because of their undesirability.

JP: What is the major difference between you and sheriffs?

A: The sheriff is a city employee on a salary of the city and as such has all the titles and benefits of a municipal employee. A city marshal is an independent contractor working with the civil court by authorization of the state law. And as such, their salary is determined by the amount of energy and effort that they put into the job. It's not very different from being self employed because one generates one's own income.

JP: How do you do that?

A: By getting clients consisting of mainly, like I said before, utilities, attorneys, landlords, management corporations, and things like that.

JP: So you solicit them or advertise?

A: No, we can't advertise. We are restricted from advertising except what goes in the yellow pages, which we're required to do. But we can't, like [the law firm] Jacoby & Myers, go on a TV spot on television and advertise our services, nor can we publish advertisements in periodicals, magazines, and newspapers.

JP: Why is that?

A: I have no idea why a lot of this stuff is. It was there when I came, and it's prevailed while I'm here, and I'm sure it will still be procedure when I'm gone. It's just that we were admonished and informed that we cannot do that. It evolved with the state law.

JP: Do you have any dealings with bounty hunters?

A: No.

JP: What are the changes that you've seen over the fourteen years you've been in business?

A: I think that my business has grown, but I don't think that reflects any sociological phenomena. I think it's just that I've been successful, and when a person is successful, their services are recommended to other people. And if you satisfy your clients, your business grows. I don't think it's directly related to anything going on in our society. It's steady, and I think that I do a good job, and I attribute that to the increase and volume of my business.

JP: What are the qualifications?

A: The completion of a twenty-seven-odd page application which asks you everything that's conceivable. And it's pursued, reviewed, and investigated by the New York City Department of Investigation. I don't know what criteria they use. They take the applications and peruse them and select, as they determine one's suitability for the position. In other words, they don't ask for educational experience specifically or a certain kind of background. As far as my knowledge is, it varies in educational backgrounds and similarly experiential backgrounds specifically. Marshals come from all walks of life.

JP: Do you have to be a citizen?

A: I would imagine, yes.

JP: Can you be an ex-offender?

A: I would think not. I would only be guessing. Of course, I'm a citizen, and I don't have a criminal record so I guess that would be important, but I don't know whether or not in the past or in the future, those who have been or will meet the selection criteria will be either in or out.

JP: How big is your staff?

A: At present, my staff fluctuates. My staff is run from as few as three to as many as five or six people.

JP: That's your administrative staff. Are they considered marshals or deputy marshals?

A:No. They are support staff.

JP: Do you know of any marshals that are female?

A: Yes.

JP: Are there many?

A: There are several that I know. I wouldn't say that there are many, but there are some that I know.

JP: What's been your most exciting or interesting case?

A: I never even considered that. I think every day is a surprise as part of the fascination of the job, the fact that it's not predictable. You never know what's on the other side of the door when you knock on it, and I guess that aspect of it for me holds my interest and keeps me getting up in the morning to continue to do this job. Many, many things have happened during the course of this job, but I can't think off hand of any singular item or incident.

JP: Well, what was the most dangerous?

A: Every day. I've gone into apartments with drug dealers. I've picked up cars when my life was threatened. You got to learn how to not be or allow yourself to be drawn into the discontent of a client or a customer or a tenant or an irate superintendent. I mean all of it is dangerous or threatens to be potentially dangerous.

JP: Does your family is approve of your work?

A: Yes.

JP: Anyone in your family in the business?

A: No.

JP: Would you want them to be?

A: I don't know. I don't think so, no.

JP: Because of the danger of it?

A: Well, it has some rewards. It has many disappointments. It is very demanding. It's not the kind of job where you have sick time or you have vacation time that you can take off. You have to plan that carefully to step away from the job because your clients always want you to be available. So, it's very, very demanding physically. It is something that one will have to be prepared to be very conscientious about, to do a good job.

JP: So, obviously your business is not 9 A.M. to 5 P.M.?

A: Oh, I wish it was in terms of executing the warrants, but that's when my work starts in the office after that. You see, I'm in my office right now. It's almost seven.

JP: What about weekends? Do you have to work on weekends, too?

A: Only when I have to come in to go over the books, review some things with staff and what not. As in terms of the formal duties, no. We can't execute warrants on the weekends or anything like that. But to catch up with my paperwork or to go over various accounts, very often on the weekends I have to do that. It's the only time I have time.

JP: Is there a lot of paperwork?

A: A lot of paperwork.

JP: And is this paperwork for the city or for your clients?

A: For the courts, for my clients, for myself, for the Department of Investigation, absolutely. I mean very, very rigid and rigorous paperwork is required. Very meticulous. It can't be happenstance. You're dealing with legal pad papers for the most part and very important issues. None of it can be treated lightly. It is a lot of very, very critical paperwork that has to be handled.

JP: When you go to execute warrants, do you go alone or do you take the police, or do you take your staff?

A: Oh, no. My staff is my office staff. I usually go alone. In some instances, police have to be called in, but not as a rule; certainly not before I assess the situation.

JP: Are people usually cooperative with you?

A: Yes.

JP: And you carry a weapon?

A: Yes.

JP: Is that part of being a city marshal or is that separate?

A: That's part of being a marshal.

JP: Automatically, when you become a marshal you can carry a weapon?

A: Yes, you can get the license.

JP: Most of your income is derived from lawyers, the city, et cetera.

A: Right.

JP: So whatever they pay you is business income?

A: Statutory fees. They are established by the state. I can't make up any fees.

JP: Can you give me a couple of examples?

A: Not off hand. There's a fee attached to everything a marshal does. He gets a certain fee for receiving information from the court. You get a fee for serving a seventy-two hour notice. You get a fee for executing a warrant of eviction. You get a fee if you're picking up cars. You get a fee for whatever it is that you do, for a bank levy. You get a fee for conducting an auction. You get a fee for inventory.

JP: You have a marshal sale.

A: Yeah. You get a fee for that.

JP: How do you execute the eviction warrant?

A: How?

JP: I mean you just hand it to them and leave or do you actually—

A: Oh no, you have to see to it that the people leave the premises.

JP: And you have to remove their possessions?

A: If it's required by the management company or the landlord, yes, you have to see that it is removed.

JP: Sometimes your client might direct you just to have the people leave, and they leave their belongings.

A: Yes.

U.S. MARSHALS

TWENTIETH-CENTURY U.S. MARSHALS

Often, city or town marshals are confused with U.S. federal marshals. As a result, a description of the U.S. Marshals Service (USM) is provided. Ample documentation exists concerning the Marshals Services' history and responsibilities. They were established long before the Federal Bureau of Investigation, and could assume the mantle of our first national police force providing judicial security, witness protection, prisoner security, (federal) fugitive investigation, and apprehension. The Marshals Service can, on the federal level, "seize and manage property under court order and take custody of cash and property. They also manage property targeted for forfeiture in judicial forfeiture actions. The service's current inventory of seized property, worth $1.8 billion, includes real estate—houses, ranches, operating businesses, apartment complexes."[1]

Federal marshals are probably our nation's hardest working law-enforcement branch as the preceding partial list of responsibilities illustrates. Additional activities encompass workshops, briefings, and training for crime fighters in other U.S. agencies: federal, state, local, as well as the law enforcers around the world. The Virginia Sheriffs

Association (VSA) and the National Workshop District Judges in New Orleans are two examples of the Marshals Service's diverse work.

For instance, a seminar was conducted for VSA emphasizing court facility maintenance, courtroom security, and bailiff training, together with personal security and organizations' protection respectively.[2] Cooperating and assisting colleagues in law implementation and enforcement (no matter how unpopular) and fugitive apprehension round out this agency's daily, myriad responsibilities. Further, they employ time-honored as well as creative strategies to apprehend criminals. From October 1981 through April 1986, the marshals service launched a massive, integrated strike force to capture long-time fugitives, some of whom had been years on the Marshals Service's most-wanted list.

Through a campaign designed and implemented by the Fugitive Investigative Strike Team (FIST), they concocted various scams to lure and capture fugitives, using such means as invitations to parties, free sports tickets, inheritance, all-expense-paid travel tickets, mail carriers delivering signature-required packages, and so on. Hundreds of fugitives were arrested. Furthermore, addresses or geographical locations of other fugitives were obtained. With the local law people's cooperation and participation, the crusade that targeted nine geographical areas was tremendously successful.[3] Marshals are exemplary law officers as well as astute in business. They manage forfeited property so successfully that the federal Office of Management and Budget (OMB) advise other agencies to adopt marshals service management procedures. A more detailed look at the twentieth-century marshals service's copious responsibilities is educational and impressive.

Investigation/Apprehension of Federal Fugitives

As the name implies, the marshals service is primarily responsible for federal prisoners, escapees, probation, parole, bail bond violators, and Drug Enforcement Administration (DEA) warrants. According to a Marshals Service 1993 fact sheet (Publication #26), marshals arrest nearly seventeen thousand fugitive felons nationwide with state and local law enforcers' assistance. Interestingly, marshals execute more fugitive arrest warrants than all federal law enforcement agencies combined (U.S. Marshals Service, *Fact Sheet No. 26*).

Prisoner Transportation

The Marshals Service, in their role of prisoner custodians, must provide transportation after an arrest and when sentenced. Transferring prisoners among institutions and states is accomplished with the assistance and cooperation of the Bureau of Prisons. To effectuate this bustling business, in 1984 the Marshals Service acquired a prisoner airline. With two Boeing 727s and several smaller jets they transport thousands of prisoners nationally. Essentially, there are no taxpayer costs for the fleet because the Marshals Service is given government surplus planes and use asset seizure and forfeiture items. Their hub in Oklahoma City "is the only government operated, scheduled passenger airline in the nation, serving thirty-seven cities."[4]

Moreover, in the American spirit of cooperation, this airline is available to law enforcement agencies throughout the country. Marshals complete "more than one hundred fifty-five thousand prison movements a year via coordinated air and ground systems."[5] The Marshals Service houses nearly twenty thousand unsentenced prisoners on a daily basis in federal, local, and state jails. Jail overcrowding is an issue in most states. As a result, the Marshals Service will improve the facilities, under the Cooperative Agreement Program, "in return for guaranteed space for federal prisoners."[6] Note that the Marshals Service has raised the art of networking to a new level.

Witness and Court Security

Movies and television have made people aware of the Federal Witness Program, thus it has a mystique attached. Whether the nation knows that the Marshals Service has responsibility for this program is questionable. The 1996 movie *Eraser* will likely educate many U.S. residents about the Marshals Service and its duties. Since 1971, over six thousand witnesses (not including family members) have become part of the federal marshals' witness security program. These people have been protected, relocated, and given new identities. In addition, the program's success can be measured by the 89 percent conviction rate achieved through protected witnesses' testimony. In turn, witnesses receive housing, medical care, job training, employment, and money at taxpayers expense.

Furthermore, the U.S. Marshals Service provides around-the-clock protection when the witness has court appearances. Court security for federal judges, court officials, nonprotected witnesses, and jurors, as well as protection away from the courtroom when needed, are in the Marshals Service's bailiwick. Over seven hundred locations throughout the nation, where federal court business is conducted, have the marshals' protection. Finally, there are the marshals' contracts regarding oversight, that is, responsibilities concerning buying, installing, and maintaining judicial security systems.

Women of color and women of European heritage have a short and recent history as U.S. marshals. Faith P. Evans of Hawaii was "the first presidentially appointed female"[7] on August 12, 1982. Frederick

Douglass was the first marshal of African descent, appointed in 1877 for the District of Columbia. The U.S. Marshals Service currently has an award in his name. Deputy Director John Twomey was its first recipient in February 1989 (United States Marshals Service, *Pentacle*, 25).

NINETEENTH-CENTURY U.S. MARSHALS

Unlike the dedicated women and men in the U.S. Marshals Service today, they were not always so professional. As the U.S. Marshals Service's history illustrates, there were unflattering eras in the service. Actually, deputy U.S. marshals, appointed by U.S. marshals, often were the brave heroes that historians have attributed to presidential appointees. Of interest are the similarities among eighteenth-century U.S. marshals and twentieth-century city marshals and even bounty hunters.

U.S. marshals whose jurisdiction were the territories of New Mexico and Arizona had their work cut out for them, to put it mildly. Like frontier sheriffs, U.S. marshals had the unenviable tasks of policing huge geographical areas. These included deserts and remote valleys inhabited primarily by lawless unemployed men looking to make a fortune and return East, as well as Native Americans struggling against the tide of Europeans bent on taking control of their land. Often marshals spent weeks in the saddle enforcing the law. Towns were small and miles apart.

When they encountered overwhelming violence, especially between the years of 1854 and 1878, U.S. marshals executed their special authority and deputized regular army units. Violent confrontations were essentially the norm. Arizona and New Mexico have consistently been characterized as the two most dangerous frontier territories. In addition, frontier judges made the marshals' jobs more difficult because the territorial judiciary was the federal law enforcement system's weakest link. Too few judges or justices of the peace had legal training and experience. Many were heavy drinkers, and too many had unsavory backgrounds. Despite these challenges, marshals and their deputies helped tame the West, bringing order as well as law.

Basically, with certain exceptions, deputy marshals performed all the work of tracking and capturing criminals. When a reward was offered, deputies usually had an agreement whereby they would split the cash with the marshals service.[8] In actuality, those deputies were bounty hunters earning their salaries through rewards and routine service fees. Also, deputy marshals sometimes served as peace officers, the only law in unorganized frontier regions. But generally the bulk of the marshals' work was civil (subpoenas, warrants, conducting property sales, locating witnesses, impaneling juries, performing various federal court tasks, etc.), rather than criminal, during the years 1789–1896.

A significant number of deputy marshals were of African descent. Those men, usually recent escapees from enslavement, had virtually no formal education and were equally heroic and effective as their colleagues. These deputy marshals' names are now part of history, among them Grant Johnson, Ike Rogers, Robert Love, Ed Robinson, Wiley Escoe, and Bass Reeves.[9] Routinely, African American deputy marshals and their bosses safeguarded the mail and railroad property.[10] They were paid on a fee system until 1896, when Congress established fixed salaries. U.S. marshals hired as many deputies as they could, thus freeing the presidential appointee to earn additional money. Deputies carried out the bulk of law enforcement activities, while marshals tended to the extensive administrative tasks. Wives played an important role: They were the office managers, and increased their work when marshals traveled. The U.S. marshal's office was virtually a family operation.

In spite of Congressional limits on the number of deputies, hiring continued until 1972 under the individual U.S. marshals auspices, at which time all hiring (and training) was permanently ensconced at the U.S. marshals' headquarters. The foregoing points are important. From its inception, the U.S. marshals had at least three loyalties: profits, their communities, and the national government. On one critical occasion, community sympathies superseded their government allegiance. Prior to the start of shooting in the Civil War, marshals in the South resigned en masse, rather than support the Union. It must be acknowledged that the marshals' appointments were, in fact, patronage jobs; thus, when southern politicians withdrew from the Union, U.S. marshals followed suit (United States Marshals Service, *Pentacle*, 7).

A look at their background offers a better understanding of why this withdrawal happened. The first U.S. marshals, in 1789, were European American property owners. Regardless of party, virtually all men were married and conservative. Working part-time, they earned fees serving federal courts' needs. These men hired deputies who, usually younger than their bosses, often were marshals' family members or connected to politicians. It became the nation's first national police force, and Congress promulgated U.S. marshals' duties in 1789. It attempted to imbue them with ideas of equal law enforcement, although these lawmen had limited authority (average citizens were suspicious of any police and military, being strong individual freedom advocates).

Hence, "Marshals . . . possessed the power to enforce these novel laws that underpinned the unity of the nation."[11] National unity has been sorely tried in several different nineteenth-century time periods, including the Civil War, Reconstruction, and labor unrest. Such political and social upheavals brought major changes to the country and the U.S. Marshals Service mandate. Their duties entailed enforcing Congress' reform laws, often unwillingly. The U.S. Marshals Service's Milton B. Duffield and William Kidder Meade were among those who became reformers despite their politics.[12]

True Story

One of the most interesting and respected U.S. marshals, Bob Paul, spent his younger years as a sheriff in small California frontier towns. He fought hard for his shrievalty, winning one close election in Pima County, Arizona, against Shibbell, and losing by a narrow margin to Shaw three years later in 1884 (Long 12). Paul was famous among gangs and criminals because he had a fondness for using a sawed-off, ten-gauge shotgun. Losing all his assets in gold mining during a brief stint away from law enforcement, Paul hired out to Wells Fargo as a guard on their stages. Advancing quickly, he was appointed a special detective, investigating criminal activities in Arizona in 1877.

That territory was known for its lawlessness. "Arizona was the wildest most lawless part of the United States at that time, with robberies occurring daily and murder quite common. Organized gangs of outlaws preyed on the stage lines, and Wells Fargo was losing many valuable shipments."[13] Paul rose to the occasion, and he gained the road agents' respect and fear. In late 1890, Paul received a U.S. marshal's appointment by President Harrison, and assumed office in March 1891.

Nonetheless, he worked only two years because of Bright's disease. After thirty years in law enforcement, he died in Tucson in 1901.[14] As the preceding section illustrates, U.S. marshals have different yet similar beginnings to town marshals. Sheriffs are the next focus. They have a truly ancient past and a very interesting present, as will be shown. The resemblances and overlappings with the previously described lawpersons are fascinating, yet the profession of Sheriff has its own uniqueness.

COUNTY SHERIFFS

TWENTIETH-CENTURY COUNTY SHERIFFS

County sheriffs of the nineteenth and twentieth centuries, in the four states on which this book focuses, have more similarities than differences in terms of responsibilities. Be it the 1800s or 1990s, sheriffs still have jurisdiction over large areas, functioning as the county law enforcement agent. Serving the courts and maintaining and administrating county jails continue to be their bailiwick.

In addition to these centuries-old duties, sheriff's departments have expanded their activities by working closer with the community. They have established specific, much needed programs. These service initiatives, such as anti-domestic violence efforts, have become vital community institutions. Children and the elderly are among the people benefiting from the sheriffs' initiatives. (See interview with Sheriff Frolich.) It is important to remember that county sheriffs' mandates are different and do not overlap with the responsibilities of the New York City sheriffs discussed in a previous chapter.

Celebrating one thousand years of service, first to the king of England and then in United States' communities, sheriffs worldwide met in York, England, to commemorate the profession's longevity. Opening ceremonies took place May 1, 1992, with activities continuing through September. As noted in *Sheriffs Magazine*, town and county sheriffs are the only elected law enforcement positions in the United States (Sattler, 6). Still, despite having given three hundred fifty years of service, the position is in danger of elimination. Hawaii actually moved forward on that issue, but the sheriffs waged a battle for reinstatement and won. In 1996, they are governor-appointed with the name sheriff intact, but they reside in Hawaii's public safety department.

Hartford County, Maryland, had a charter proposal containing a repeal of the sheriff, "outlining the duties of a police chief under the heading department of police, will be added" (*Sheriff*, 25). The measure was defeated. From the beginning, Polk County, Iowa, was concerned about the legality of a charter proposal restructuring county government as well as abolishing the elected sheriff's position. Again the sheriffs secured a victory. In spite of these challenges, sheriffs are going about their normal duties and initiating much needed community focused activities. Consequently, county sheriffs nearly equal state troopers in authority and esteem as the second highest policing body. In many rural areas, sheriffs are the only local law—and the most democratic, proponents argue.

Further, these twentieth-century crime fighters increasingly reflect the population that they serve by hiring un- or underrepresented personnel. Nonetheless, this overdue embrace of forward-looking policies has catapulted sheriffs' departments into the limelight, as well as modernity, with much fanfare. To wit, an Arizona sheriff was a defendant in a 1983 sex discrimination law suit. He publicly called his former deputy, "a dingbat, little gal" and observed that "women were unfit for work out in the field." The plaintiff's attorney, Mr. Schleir, said the settlement, $405,000, was large because the sheriff's actions and those of other supervisors were "blatant and flagrant." The plaintiff also complained that an uncertified, inexperienced man received full-time deputyship, even though she had state certification and two years experience (*Star*, 12). Often, initiatives designed as a beacon for future generations can bring conflict and hostility.

However, change is inevitable. It should be embraced, not resisted. Law enforcement and jail maintenance are contemporary sheriffs' two primary functions. They have become completely diversified. Having performed the above duties since colonial days, a significant number of modern sheriffs have moved forward into the twenty-first century, instituting child safety programs, community policing, senior citizen identification programs, and in Union County, New Jersey, Operation Bread Basket.

New York State's sheriffs operate a scholarship project, as well as an anti-drug initiative, together with work-site health and fitness promotions to reduce stress among their officers. In sum, sheriffs' research, training, program implementation, and technical assistance may soon replace traditional duties. Concomitantly, county jails and prisoner administration do continue to be the sheriffs' fundamental responsibilities, along with court and other judicial services, like executing court papers and property forfeiture. Of interest is the removal of comprehensive jail administration from some sheriffs' jurisdiction, which sounds an ominous chord, as their supporters note.

Sheriffs are rightly worried about those expanding efforts seeking to abrogate the office. Moreover, a few critics have voiced disapproval of law officers operating jails. They maintain that the deputy sheriffs' approach to penal institutions is informed by enforcement pedagogy rather than correction. Another reason jail operations have come under scrutiny is the campaign for privatizing correctional institutions. Such efforts are gaining momentum around the country because of budget short-falls. In this corporate win-win situation, those initiatives leave sheriffs and deputies without daily jail responsibilities. In other words, budgetary attacks on the sheriffs' office continue through considerations of remanding civil processing to private entrepreneurs, like New York City's use of entrepreneurial marshals.

Regardless of traditional jail administration responsibilities, sheriffs, as outlined previously, have implemented community projects that virtually surpass those in nonelected enforcement departments. Yet, the sheriffs' dedication to policing, together with sanctions, is stronger than ever. Innovation flourishes in this research's four designated states, not all of which can be considered a community enhancement strategy. To illustrate, an Arizona sheriff substitutes the infamous "neutra" loaf at meal time to unruly prisoners. (During a telephone interview, it was explained that the neutra loaf contained all the day's food rations ground up and baked.) He acknowledged that federal guides prohibited withholding meals. Hence, the loaf, although food, was punishment because the inmates hated it. On the positive and humane side, a New Jersey sheriff suspends evictions during the Christmas holiday season.

True Story

On April 27, 1992, a group of American sheriffs and their spouses, including National Sheriffs Association President Frank Policaro Jr., sheriff of Beaver County, Pennsylvania, and Sheriff Ted Sattler, Lancaster County, Pennsylvania, traveled to England to represent the sheriffs of the United States in the celebration of the millennium of the Office of High Sheriff. During their nine-day trip, the American entourage met with past, present, and future high sheriffs of England and Wales, and learned much about the proud and colorful history of the sheriff. The following conversation took place in the bar of the Copthorne Tara Hotel, London, on the evening of their arrival to observe the celebration of the sheriff's millennium:

Barman (Bartender): Wot'll it be, gents?

Sheriff Sattler: A pint of your best bitter, please, and a Shirley Temple for my friend, Sheriff Policaro.

Barman: Right-O! I say, are you men sheriffs? American sheriffs? What smashing badges! Welcome to England. Are you 'ere to arrest someone?

Sheriff Policaro: No, we're here to participate in the sheriffs millennium in England. This is the one-thousandth year of the office of the high sheriff in your country, and we're here to help them celebrate.

Barman: Help who celebrate?

Sheriff Sattler: Your sheriffs.

Barman: Wot sheriffs?

Sheriff Policaro: Your sheriffs—your high sheriffs!

Barman: You're putting me on, right?

Sheriff Sattler: No, indeed. The Duke of York is even dedicating a train to them.

Barman: To whom? Our sheriffs? Blimey, I didn't know we had any! Where are they?

Sheriff Policaro: They're all over Great Britain. Didn't you know that?

Barman: Lor' luv me, no! Is that straight up? Hey, Charlie, come 'ere and listen to this. Did'ja know we still 'ave sheriffs 'ere in England?

Unbelievable, you say? In the country that originated the office of sheriff? Nevertheless, it's true. English sheriffs have metamorphosed from one of the most powerful and influential offices in the land—capable of raising an army, levying taxes, adjudicating life or death, in complete control of a shire or county, answerable only to their monarch—into one that is largely ceremonial in nature. How did this happen? Well, it's quite a story. The establishment of large municipal police forces hastened the sheriffs' loss of power and stature.

Edited Interview: Sheriff Ralph Froehlich—Union County,
New Jersey

JP: Please tell me about your background.

Sheriff Froehlich: I'm the sheriff here for eighteen years. And in my nineteenth year now I was just elected to my seventh consecutive term. People have been good to me, but law enforcement has been even better. I wouldn't be here if I wasn't a policeman first because that's when I really learned service. Sadly, today too many of us look at the policemen, both the public and the police, look at the police person as the law enforcer instead of the public servant. Today, you say to the police officer, you're a public servant or you're a social worker, why, they get all bent out of shape. But truly, in my opinion, that's what a good police officer is. He's a public servant, and he is a social worker, and he is an enforcer. He wears many hats. And the public needs you to portray that image to wear all of those hats at various times. Once the public narrows down and sees you only as the enforcer, you're in trouble. Once the officer narrows his function down and sees himself as only the enforcer, not the teacher, not the helper, not the guide, then he's degrading himself.

JP: Why do you think the profession changed?

Sheriff: Our society changed.

JP: And do you think there will be a return to the old ways of policing?

Sheriff: No, I don't. Not the way we're moving today. There was a time when the functions of a family, church, and the schools were important. Those, in my opinion, are the columns that support society. If we have a good family around us, if we have a good school system, and certainly if we have a good family, we're going to have good church-going people. And that doesn't mean you go to church every Sunday. It means you know the basics. It means you're taught respect. It means you're taught the commandments. And those three things are just absolutely paramount. We have lost them all. We've lost our family. We've lost our religious institutions. As a result, we've lost control of our schools. And as a result of all this, we've lost control of our streets and the population of our young people. Shame on us for allowing that to happen. It was easier to do years ago because we had more walking police officers. When I walked my post, I knew almost everybody on my post. I knew every store on my post. I could stop in any place on a cold day and have a cup of tea or a cup of coffee. If children came by and were a little rowdy or whatever, as soon as they saw me, there was a stop.

Today, when our juveniles see the police officer they show even more aggression and put a show on for their friends and associates. In the old days, anybody say, "Hey, yeah, I want to talk to you." And we would talk. And I said, "Gee, I just saw Jackie. She really wasn't doing something really bad." "Thanks, Ralph, I'll take care of it." Today, even if Jackie is doing something seriously wrong, and I go home and tell Jackie's parents, there's almost a confrontation. "Why are you picking on my Jackie?" Especially if Jackie is a minority. Not the way to respond. The policeman has been asked to be the servant to these communities and has to run past wealth or poverty. Now he has to run past color. Granted, you also have to be sensitive to certain areas where you might have to put a little effort into understanding the different people on your post. My old post, I had Ukrainians, Russians, Hispanics, and big black population. I worked in what they called the ghetto.

JP: Did they know the cop on the beat by name?

Sheriff: Absolutely, knew us as Ralph, knew us as Moe, knew as Owen. We were respected. We were liked. Which wasn't easy for somebody like myself because I kind of stood out. I was the minority then. And I know a lot of our people today don't like to hear this, but there was racism. There was awareness of color when I was policeman. When I went to the radio car with my partner, we were what they called one of the first "salt and pepper" teams which means match a black officer with a white officer. There were geographical boundaries, not in writing, but there were geographical boundaries because I was working with a black officer. You didn't go above that location. Not so today. That's all gone.

JP: Do you think that if officers return to walking the beat, things will improve between the community and the police?

Sheriff: Absolutely. There must be contact with your people. It's going to take an awful lot. I'm an elected official now. I got into politics because I didn't like politicians. That's fact.

JP: You didn't like them or you didn't trust them?

Sheriff: No, I didn't, both, other than a few people that I've come to know. I've come to know some very fine people—Democrats, Republicans irrelevant—just some nice people. You will see elected officials campaigning prior to election, on crime issues—we have to do something about crime in the street, crime becomes whatever, I'm going to do this, this, and that. And that's all great until the day after election. Then they forget about it. If I talk to you or your students and you talk about preventive medicine, prevention of AIDS, prevention of heart disease, prevention of cancer—it's all understandable, we all comprehend that. But if I talk to you about crime prevention, which veteran police officers have emphasized for thirty and forty years, some people still don't want to hear it.

JP: Why is that?

Sheriff: Money. Money, hard-nosed, and acceptability. They don't want to put the money out.

JP: What are the differences in the professions, sheriff and police officer? I didn't know until a few minutes ago that you were a cop on the beat. What are the differences between the two sets of responsibilities?

Sheriff: I tried to bring my experience as a street cop into this office. When I first came here nineteen or twenty years ago, sheriffs in the state of New Jersey had very little to do with the public. They served papers, they took care of the court security, and didn't do a lot of crime prevention. They weren't a servant of the people, they were the servant of the courts. I think a lot of us, a lot of new sheriffs, have worked at changing this. That we have become more the teacher, the advisor, and the resource. I think you heard me when I first came in talking to a man about domestic violence. That's a very important part of our work today.

JP: Domestic violence?

Sheriff: Oh, absolutely. We are the only agency in the entire state of New Jersey to have a special domestic violence unit.

JP: Did you say the only one in the state?

Sheriff: Yep! The only one in the state. We have a special unit where one of my officers, Detective Sharon Getts, a very fine lady, rides in a radio car in the city of Elizabeth with a patrolman. When there is a domestic violence incident, they immediately respond and evaluate it. Primary interest, of course, is safety. Sometimes with their expertise, they can guide these people to get help where it doesn't further hurt the marriages. If the incident is serious enough where you sit down with the defendant, you sit down with the plaintiffs, sit down with the woman, and help her go through all of the paperwork, which is lengthy. The woman is usually very upset and hesitant because she usually has children and is concerned what is going to take place. So my officer sits down and even at midnight has instant contact with the judge. This is due to her awareness of the court policy, which that works out very, very well for us. It worked out so well that I just expanded it to two units of boundaries in our county.

JP: Which ones?

Sheriff: Elizabeth, New Jersey, and the new one is Plainfield, New

Jersey. I chose Plainfield because our records indicate that's where the highest number of incidents take place. First was Elizabeth, and Plainfield was second. Now I would like to expand it to a third one, but as I mentioned before there is a funding issue. I have three women on the Freeholder Board. I went to them four consecutive years asking for help on domestic violence knowing that this would be ideal. No woman, especially in authority, is going to say to Ralph, "No." Yet, I got absolutely no help four years in a row for domestic violence. Domestic violence costs. That's a fact. And yet the same people will campaign for women's right, et cetera.

JP: So, twenty years ago the sheriffs in New Jersey primarily served the courts.

Sheriff: Yes.

JP: Currently, a substantial aspect of sheriff's responsibilities include developing community programs.

Sheriff: Oh, there are all kinds of activity throughout the whole state.

JP: But are these initiatives legal requirements or by regulation?

Sheriff: No, it's legal. And I gave you copies of the brochure. One of the things I was able to implement about eighteen years ago was the change from the title of court attendant, which limited you to working for the courts, to the civil service title of sheriff's officer. Once you became the sheriff's officer it just opened up all of the other activities you could take.

JP: Just by a name change, how was that civil service title obtained?

Sheriff: There are two civil service titles—one is court attendant and one is sheriff's officer. Court attendant was very restrictive; we did nothing. You got the judge's coffee in the morning, you cashed his check on Thursday, and you helped him put his robes on, and you opened the windows for him. That was kind of dumb to put money out for that kind of an investment. It wasn't fair because you were a law enforcement officer. You weren't doing much law enforcement here.

JP: Let's go back to court attendant and being realistic.

Sheriff: Well, that change opened up the doors. You see, the sheriff's officer title is a civil service job. So they have to take a test for it. That means it's opened to anybody who wants to take that test. Now the challenge of the administrator is the selection process. That's the challenge.

JP: So your duty as the sheriff of Union County in this day and age is primarily administrative?

Sheriff: Yes.

JP: What are your law enforcement powers?

Sheriff: Everything that a police officer does. Absolutely wide open. The only addition that I have, I represent the entire county where the local policeman only goes into one city. I can go to twenty-one municipalities and function.

JP: So you have jurisdiction over . . . ?

Sheriff: Five hundred thousand people.

JP: Roselle Park?

Sheriff: Roselle, Roselle Park, Linden, Elizabeth.

JP: Can people call the sheriff and not call the Roselle police?

Sheriff: The municipality is the response. The local police respond to the specific incident.

JP: Residents have to go through them first?

Sheriff: Yes.

JP: So an ordinary person couldn't bypass the municipal people?

Sheriff: No. Also, I don't have marked units on the road. Most sheriffs don't. There are only two counties, I think, that have marked units on the road to respond to incidents, and I think one is in Bergen County, but I'm not sure about other one. But in general we do not do day-to-day responses to the automobile accident, the burglary, hold up in progress. We don't do that.

JP: Are you on a higher level than a city police?

Sheriff: Yes. Of course, our jurisdiction goes through the entire county.

JP: When would you be called for a local mission? When would you be called to, say, supersede city police?

Sheriff: We're a resource in municipalities. For instance, this is our search and rescue unit. Search and rescue unit is a nice way of saying canine unit. We've changed the name because realistically canine was kind of a . . . it wasn't a pleasant term. Because most of our people would look at the term canine and think about the Martin Luther King demonstrations, and see demonstrators and the police dogs and the negative image that was conveyed at that time. So to make it more salable you change it to search and rescue because that's semantics, and police work is salesmanship very often. Roselle, Elizabeth, Linden, Springfield—they don't have their own dogs. They don't have a search and rescue unit until they call us, and then my officers respond and utilize whatever dog happens to be necessary whether it's a bomb scare, search for narcotics, search for missing persons or senior citizens, drug search, or search for somebody in the building because I have the dogs that do all those different things. So that's what we are, a resource.

JP:But you could respond on your own to a case in the city?

Sheriff: Oh, absolutely. I could, but that's not the way to work. That's not the way to have good relationships between your municipalities and your sheriff. Because I was a policeman for so many years, I know so many of the other chiefs today. So there's a good working relationship. Today, things have changed a great deal.

JP: Let's examine the hierarchy. You have the municipal police at the law enforcement base.

Sheriff: Right. Next, the county sheriff and the state police and then federal agents.

JP: Your basic responsibility is still serving the court.

Sheriff: Oh, yes, ma'am. The primary function is court security. You still are an arm of the courts. In our county in February, I just got the report yesterday, we moved 2,454 inmates throughout this courthouse complex. But the sheriff in Union County has nothing to do with the jail. Freeholders run it.

JP: Was this always their function?

Sheriff: The sheriff used to run it. The freeholders, as a political move, took the jail away from the sheriff in 1981, and they have regretted it ever since because they have had nothing but problems with it.

JP: And that's just Union County?

Sheriff: In the state of New Jersey I would say two-thirds of jails are not run by sheriffs.

JP: Two-thirds?

Sheriff: Yes, approximately. It doesn't make sense with the interaction of the jails and the courts daily not to be under one director. I don't care if Ralph Froehlich is the sheriff or you're the sheriff or whatever. Administratively, the expertise is there. Politically, unfortunately that's how things are. But one of my primary functions is still court security.

That's a very sensitive area, court security, because realizing your handicap with an inmate, with a defendant I should say, concerning security, he or she is in the public view, actually, is in the view of the jurors. You can't let your security indicate to the jurors that this is a dangerous person because you're then influencing the juror. So it's very difficult to have subtle security, not to overstaff the uniforms. That's a challenge for our officers.

JP: How do you meet that challenge?

Sheriff: The quality of your officers, the design of your courtrooms, the electronic security devices, which are cameras, but the primary thing again comes down to your officer, quality officers, good training, good selection, and then good retraining. And a philosophy.

JP: Which is?

Sheriff: All people want is fairness and respect. You don't put your hands on anybody. You don't embarrass them in front of their families. Paramount, do not embarrass men in front of their families or on the corner, that's going to cause you grief. You don't do that. You don't go into the Vatican City to arrest the pope. You wait until he comes out. I mean, it's just common sense. However, if somebody raises his hand to you as to hurt you, and I support my officers with this 100 percent, you do what you have to do. You do it quickly because I will not tolerate my officers being a punching bag for anybody. Nobody. As a result, the word has gotten around about our officers. You work fair with the guys, they'll give you a break. Guaranteed, if a guy's a turkey, they don't care where he comes from. He's going to be a habitual. If I give him a break today, he's a turkey, he's going to come around in circle again. I've done this in the streets, so I know it works. I did it from when I was a young police officer.

JP: Tell me about the training, particularly the candidate selections. What attributes are the most prized?

Sheriff: My original selection process is this. You've got five people, and they've all passed the state exam. They're all civil servants. I get a list from civil service. I have to work off that list. The challenge to me is not the hiring process. It's when you deal with civil service. It's very, very difficult. We do a background investigation. When my office has finished a background investigation on you, I can tell you how many times you were late for grammar school. I know you. When we send you for a psychiatric exam, because the law enforcement officer has a tremendous amount of power, legal power and then force. He carries weapons, he carries that badge, it is a tremendous amount of power they have. You give me a nice person, I can teach you everything else. I don't need a hot shot. Then we do an oral interview along with our physical exam.

JP: You mentioned a few minutes ago about the oral interview. What are some of the things you ask and what are some of the things you find out?

Sheriff: Racial things that you find out in an oral interview. Preferences. Reaction. And very honestly, sometimes, not sometimes, we do, we will stack the deck on you. We will have somebody, we will have sheriff's officer, the sheriff's sergeant, a lieutenant, and possibly one of my underheriffs. So there are a variety of levels there. I don't know where we stand legally, but we do it anyhow and it works. We'll have somebody there that we needle on racial issues. If I have a white candidate coming in, for instance, I may set him or her up. Say what the Hell we're doing. What do you think of this so and so comes up and swear at you or hit you. Or, if I use a term and I want to see what kind of a reaction, and certainly I understand the intimidation of Harry Smith wanting a job. But what you can see in body language, you can see is he comfortable when I said that. Did he join quickly? And then you look deeper into his remarks. Is he prejudiced? On my force, I hire men and women who can work with everybody. And they must perform their duties in the community fairly and without bias, or answer to me.

JP: Do you have to okay raids?

Sheriff: For my agency, yes. Very often. I probably go on 95 percent of the raids. Not that I'm that much help, but my staff likes to see me there. They want to know that I am interested. And then it helps out when I have a critique. We have a critique after every raid.

JP: Does training figure in this post-raid session?

Sheriff: Constantly. That's why when I stay that close, I don't get intimidated if some attorney walks through the door with a piece a paper in his hand of an allegation of excessive use of force. No. Police brutality stuff. I can have them walk in and sit down, let him do his spiel, and then look at the officers. Well, let's see this is officer so-and-so, and officer so-and-so. Sometimes I read the names. Then I'll get their report and see what the report says. No, not these officers.

JP: What else does the department do?

Sheriff: We'll do a county raid twice a year looking for deadbeat dads. Deadbeat dad means someone who does not support his children.

JP: Right. What does a county raid entail?

Sheriff: County raid means we'll dig out the warrants for every municipality and distribute them, or have a special assault group, a unit to go to each municipality. All those working might have two or three units going. Berkeley Heights we probably wouldn't have any because Berkeley Heights doesn't have any warrants. Plainfield would probably have two. Roselle one.

JP: You do it all at once?

Sheriff: We do it all at once.

JP: Do you have to have cooperation of the local police?

Sheriff: Oh, yes. For that kind of a raid, yes. Or it's a drug raid, then everything has to be coordinated. Because if we're going to get people throughout the entire county, we don't want to get you at 1:00 and then wait 'til 3:00 where you can get a chance to make a telephone call and tell the rest of your friends. So it's all coordinated.

JP: What do sheriffs and deputies do day-to-day?

Sheriff: It starts off with our court security. Along with our court security, transporting and maintaining the security of the defendant is certainly paramount. The court security also means the environment in the court complex, which is three different buildings. And when you came in you probably saw you had to walk through the electronic device. Every package, every piece of mail goes through that electronic device. Every person who walks into this complex, a million people a year, has to go in and out of that electronic device. It's unfortunate, but those are the facts that exist today. By the way, I am dead set against privatization for any of those functions. Absolutely, dead set against it. You want professional people selected by you, trained by you, and you're responsible, you're accountable. We also transport from the county jail. Even though we have nothing to do with the jail, we transport all the prisoners from this jail to the state facilities. We also transport everybody.

JP: After the trial?

Sheriff: Yes, if they're found guilty and sentenced, then we transport you to either Rahway or Trenton or wherever.

JP: You stop at the gate, your jurisdiction stops there?

Sheriff: That's it. Then it's up to the state. We also do all the transportations if an inmate becomes ill and needs—

JP: In the jail, not the prison?

Sheriff: In the jail, county jail.—and needs dialysis, needs a dentist, we take that prisoner to the dentist, and we're accountable for his security there, which is very challenging.

JP: City jail means city cops.

Sheriff: Right. And usually in a city jail, you stay overnight, and that's it and then you go up to the county. Another very sensitive area, as I said. Freeholders run the county jails. Dumb! Dumb! Of course, we do all the extraditing. I don't know if you recall a guy named John List, killed his mother, his wife, and his three children in Westfield, New Jersey, escaped. He was on *America's Most Wanted*. He escaped, and he went to Virginia. To bring him back here, that's my job or the job of my office. We went down to pick him up in Virginia, and then transported him safely back here. That's sensitive because you're in the public airports, limited security, so that's very, very hard to do. Our search and rescue unit, which, of course, is our dogs. We have dogs that search the route before the president arrives in Union County and other counties. Our search and rescue unit is the training area.

JP: How are you feeling when you know your staff is well trained, but you have to work with staff people from other agencies whose personnel may be minimally prepared?

Sheriff: I worry a little bit. Fortunately, I can say I only worry a little bit because in our county I know a lot of chiefs. Since I was a patrolman I would say the vast majority of our chiefs are pretty decent guys that truly want to do a job. I will say this to you. I was asked to do the same thing with the jail a couple of years ago.

JP: What?

Sheriff: If they had an incident inside the jail, how would we support them?

JP: With the freeholders input?

Sheriff: Yes. And my response did not make the freeholders very happy. See, I won't go into the jail with my officers. I refused. I said I'll take care of the outside. I will transport for you. I won't go inside and jeopardize my officers because you don't do the same training that we do. I told them that.

JP: You made a lot of friends with that stand.

Sheriff: The jail administrator sat right there when I said no. I'll cover outside for you and I'll give you the support you need outside. Now, I would change my opinion on that if at some time in the future we had coordinated drills together, where we worked on things together, where we had interaction. See, I don't have a problem working with the FBI or the marshal's office Elizabeth or Plainfield officers because my people have been working with them for years, and we know one another. We know how we work. We feel confident with one another. We know the men and women by name, by sight. I'm not going to do that and jeopardize my trained officers with somebody who may not feel as confident. And if you're not confident, that's when you resort to force. Fear, very often, is the root. If you're confident, you're less apt to do violence.

JP: Previously, you mentioned the marshals, and I was glad that you did because I'm also doing research on them. Are there any city or town marshals?

Sheriff: United States marshals only. There are no town marshals.

JP: So you work with United States marshals?

Sheriff: Oh, yes.

JP: How?

Sheriff: Raids. The raids are for fugitives.

JP: So, city police don't get involved?

Sheriff: When the United States marshal forms a strike force, he may ask for cooperation from the sheriff and the local police. And just put a big task force together and go out on raids.

JP: And when the United States marshals put together a raid, the hierarchy is structured that they're in charge?

Sheriff: They're in charge, yes.

JP: When you put a county raid together, your people are in charge?

Sheriff: Yes, either me or the prosecutor. The prosecutor is the chief law enforcement officer in the county. The prosecutor is very, very powerful. The prosecutor is appointed by the governor for a five-year term.

JP: And your term is?

Sheriff: My term is three years. Now, I get my commission, my authority from the attorney general of the state. The prosecutor in reality is the true boss of all law enforcement in the county, whether it's county, city, whatever, other than the state. Within his county, the prosecutor is the top law enforcement officer in the county.

JP: Do you have contacts among bail people and bounty hunters?

Sheriff: Yes. The bail process by statute is supposed to be performed by the agency that controls that body. The body meaning the prisoner. That is what the statute reads. However, when the freeholders took over the jail, they never took over that process here in Union County. My people still do the bail process across the street.

JP: Describe the bail process.

Sheriff: Everybody is entitled to bail. In our system, people are considered innocent until proven guilty. We're one of the only nations, I think, that has that. Everybody else . . . I was in China a couple years ago, and I saw their system. Interesting system. But because you're considered innocent until proven guilty, the bail is supposed to guarantee your appearance for the court hearing. The function of bail is not supposed be punishment. The only function of bail is supposed to be to guarantee your appearance in court. The bounty hunter or the bondsman has more freedom than a police officer. If you commit a crime here in Union County and take off to Connecticut or wherever, that bondsman can go after you. Find you. He does not need any paperwork from that state of Connecticut to bring you back. Put his leg irons on you. Throws you in the trunk of his car and back he comes. That's it. It's interesting law. But that's the way the law is. If we have to go pick you up, we need all kinds of extradition papers, there are legal maneuvers we have to go through.

Sheriff: This is Lieutenant Barry Migliore, in the sheriff's office.

Migliore: Even once we do have the guy, he has a right to elect not to come back with us, and it's a formal court proceeding where he either awaits extradition or not. Once in front of the judge, if he says, "Judge, I'm not going to waive extradition," and the judge says, "Okay, you don't have to go back," we have to get a governor's warrant and force him to come back.

Sheriff: Now the bounty hunter doesn't have to do that. There was a time when we didn't look on the bounty hunters too kindly. I think, Barry, in the last couple of years, you've developed some pretty good guidelines and a relationship where we do have a relationship. We do work together now. We help one another. But we won't tolerate anything less than what's appropriate. You have to set your own guidelines.

JP: What are the guidelines?

Migliore: Well basically, the bondsmen work for the people who post the bail. They have absolutely nothing to do with the sheriff's office at all. Their interest is strictly to get the money back.

JP: How many bondspersons are there, and do they work with you?

Migliore: Probably thousands. Okay. They do not work as our agents at all. They're out there strictly on their own. They have their own agents. Their interests parallel ours. Okay. The only relationship that we're both interested in is this guy being arrested and brought back to New Jersey. We have the way we do things. We can't impose them on them. But as the sheriff told you, we definitely do not cooperate with agencies that are not a legitimate business. Anybody can go and get or apply for a license, but it doesn't mean that we're going to cooperate or deal with them or give them any kind of information. We cannot give them information we have. Because then it could be construed that they're working as our agent. So we try to be real careful that way. Like the sheriff said, if they call and ask, "do you have a warrant on this guy? We have notification from the court," we'll say, yes, the warrant is open and things like that.

JP: What guidelines do you have with bounty hunters?

Migliore: We have none.

Sheriff: Do you mean how do they get appointed?

JP: No. Is there a set procedure they must follow when they contact you?

Sheriff: Jackie, I think what we have here is personal contact. People will talk to Barry. And again he makes decisions, and I encourage him. And that's what's nice here also. Barry knows how I feel, and we have very, very similar interests in our profession. There are people who come to us from legitimate bail agencies, and we know the family.

Edited Telephone Interview: James Plousis—Sheriff of Cape May County, New Jersey

JP: Please introduce yourself.

Plousis: I'm Sheriff James Plousis. The sheriff of Cape May County. I'm in my twelfth year of being sheriff in Cape May County. I'm finishing up my fourth term.

JP: How many years are there to a term?

Plousis: There are three year terms in New Jersey.

JP: What made you go into law enforcement?

Plousis: I have a bachelor of arts degree in history. I was a seasonal officer when going to college. When I graduated college, the chief asked me if I would like to stay on the police force, and at that time I didn't have any other job opportunities. So I stayed on the Ocean City police force where I was an officer there for ten years. When I was there I was assigned to the traffic division. I was also in charge of community relations. So I was familiar with the office of sheriff, and I thought more could be done at that office to assist local police.

JP: Such as?

Plousis: Some regional services that I thought could be addressed better done at the county level. For example, canine services, which we've been able to provide. Crime prevention programs could be done better at a county-based level, which we've been able to do. Countywide crime stopper tips phone line, we were able to do that. These are the items I ran my campaign on, and we were able to institute them after the election.

JP: What are your responsibilities in 1996?

Plousis: I'm a 136 personnel operation. One hundred eleven of them are sworn officers. I run a 200 bed jail facility. We run a court security unit. We have four sitting judges that we provide security for as well as anybody coming to the courts. We do fugitive apprehension where we have officers out everyday arresting people for any violation: violation of probation, criminal warrants, or child support. We do legal services from superior court as well as foreclosure sales, which, you know, has been a sheriff's function since the Magna Carta. We do that. We do crime prevention throughout the county. We have a crime prevention unit that includes crime fighting dogs. I have a canine unit of ten dogs that cover every area—bomb dog, arson dog, narcotic detection dog, patrol dog, and tracking dog—that are available to any law enforcement agency in the region. In addition to that we do communications for nine small law enforcement agencies in the county. We patrol county property. We have a large park system in the county. We have officers assigned in those parks. In addition to that we have units in the park—horses. We have a victims' service unit where we handle the notification of a victim when somebody's getting released from jail on a variety of offenses. Plus we do educational programs on victims services. We have a large emphasis on child safety. We do the child fingerprinting yearly, and we have programs where we bring children to the jail to show them the end result of drug use.

JP: Are you a process server?

Plousis: Yes. We also serve legal documents. We are a full service operation. We have officers doing all law enforcement functions as well as jail functions and as well as judicial functions in that we do transport jurors if that need arises as well. So we are a multifaceted operation.

JP: Did I hear you say that you are responsible for the jails? And that's county jails?

Plousis: Yes.

JP: Compare those functions that you just listed with, say, ten years ago.

Plousis: Let me just footnote. There is one other function. We do run a juvenile boot camp for youthful offenders. A residential boot camp for twenty days every summer. So, in addition to our traditional functions, we also run a juvenile boot camp, which is a little unique. There are only ten of them in the country, but we do run one of them out of the sheriff's office.

JP: How did you manage to get that unique program funded?

Plousis: We were very innovative. I pleaded with the Coast Guard for a number of years to allow me to use their facility. They have been kind enough to give us the facility at no cost. We went to the Marshals Service for surplus uniforms from the military.

JP: Now that's the United States marshals?

Plousis: United States marshals because I do hold federal prisoners.

JP: How about other sheriffs in New Jersey? Do they do the same thing?

Plousis: Yes, there are a number of sheriffs in New Jersey that have federal contracts. In my time as being sheriff, I've held a number of mobsters for the FBI. Nicky Scarfo I've held on three different occasions. Brady Phileonetti. I held two of the people that blew up the World Trade Center building in New York.

JP: How did they get there? In Cape May?

Plousis: They were apprehended in North Wildwood. We held them in our facility.

JP: There wasn't any place closer to New York?

Plousis: No, we are the only federal facility in the southern part of the state for the FBI, Immigration, or federal agencies.

JP: What about the northern part?

Plousis: I believe the sheriff of Bergen has a similar arrangement with the Marshals Service who hold federal prisoners.

JP: How has this office changed?

Plousis: Law enforcement has changed. Needs have changed. We've been trying to address those changes. As things evolve, as the economics get tighter and tighter in government, there's more emphasis on regionalization or sharing resources. So we've been a nucleus for that kind of operation. As I said with canine, we are the only canine service in the county. That saves the municipalities from funding their own canine, and plus it gives me the flexibility to use them in our jail operations. It's a good utilization of staffing. In addition, and at the same thing in the area of communications, running a communications center gets expensive. Hook-ups are expensive. We've been able to provide that service for the smaller agencies that can't do it on their own. What we've seen in the last twelve years is looking at things, how to be a little more effective and a little more cost savings in areas, and we've been able to move along and address that.

JP: Can you compare or differentiate for me the duties that you have as sheriff as opposed to the regular police forces in your area?

Plousis: Local police are charged with the direct policing of their municipalities and enforcing criminal law there. We do not have direct policing responsibilities in the municipalities. As you know, in New Jersey, there are no county unincorporated areas like there are in other states that give the sheriff an automatic patrol area. The only thing we have is county property in our park systems and the county buildings which we do police. So that's our direct policing involvement in the county property. Our functions at the next level of law enforcement in regards to fugitive apprehension, you know, where we arrest people throughout the county on warrants: parole warrants, probation warrants, child support warrants, or criminal warrants. We do those functions. The extradition of inmates—if somebody's arrested in another state—we do go out and get them. In addition to that, as I say the next level of functions, you know, we run the county identification bureau. Everybody arrested, we have records of them and the history of the county, their photographs, and their fingerprints. Our canine services, again, are there for the municipalities as well as our staffing. If there's an emergency in these municipalities, we're there to help them. The role of the local police is distinctly different in that they do the direct policing in those communities, and the sheriff doesn't do that in New Jersey. We offer secondary and support services more in general and, of course, administering the county jail is a different function that 93 percent of the sheriffs have in the United States. It's the exception that the sheriff doesn't run the jail. And that exception does exist in New Jersey in a few counties, but does make for, I believe, a more comprehensive system when one agency runs the entire gamut of transporting, arresting, and housing inmates.

JP: Do you do evictions?

Plousis: Yes. Of course, that is a court order. We are the enforcement arm of superior court in New Jersey. And we do a number of evictions that where a smaller county of ninety-five thousand people, we might only average one or two a year. We do that, again, on a court order.

JP: Do you have constables?

Plousis: In our county, no.

JP: That's interesting because you know they operate in North Jersey.

Plousis: They got them in other counties. But, no, we handle all the legal services in the county. That's one uniqueness of the office that it can adjust to different demographics and different geographic needs of each county. I'll give you an example. We also have a big search and rescue unit. Eighty percent of our county is rural and wetlands. So we had missing people, either elderly or small children, and we have a unit that is trained in search and rescue. It's needed in Cape May County, but in other urban areas in New Jersey, it wouldn't be needed. The sheriff has that flexibility to fill areas that need to be addressed.

JP: Do you have an undersheriff?

Plousis: I have two undersheriffs.

JP: What are their responsibilities?

Plousis: Our organization is broken into two divisions.

JP: You're elected, but they are appointed.

Plousis: Appointed by myself. We have two divisions. One is the correctional division that handles jail matters, and then we have a legal division that handles legal and law enforcement matters.

JP: And what are their terms?

Plousis: They serve with the sheriff's office and the sheriffs that have been here with me.

JP: Have you seen any change in terms of the crimes committed during your tenure versus a number of years ago?

Plousis: Yeah, there's no question. In my career, I've been in law enforcement twenty-two years, I can remember drugs were a rarity. We very seldom arrested anybody for drugs. As a matter of fact, I can remember policemen who had never seen drugs in the mid-seventies. That has changed dramatically. The drug arrests, I don't know if you're aware of this, but 70 percent of all people in custody in New Jersey today are there because of drug use or sales, were committing a crime while under the influence of drugs.

JP: This situation basically mirrors the rest of the country.

Plousis: So if any trend jumps out it is that the increase of drug use and the proportion that have increased the jail populations.

JP: In general, crime has also increased?

Plousis: Yes. Crime has increased, not as dramatically as the jail population. The jail population has doubled in the last ten years. Crime hasn't doubled in the last ten years.

JP: Why is that?

Plousis: We were seeing more mandatory sentencing. It has kept more people in jail, and that's the direct cause of that.

JP: Anyone else in your family in law enforcement?

Plousis: No.

JP: Your family approve or support your being in law enforcement?

Plousis: My family's been very supportive. My wife and children, as well as my parents, have always been supportive.

JP: Sheriff, you know I'm also writing about bounty hunters. Do you have any dealings with them?

Plousis: No. As a matter of fact, in my entire career, being a city policeman and being county sheriff, I don't ever remember running into one. I guess they're more active in the urban areas, not the rural counties. I have never had any contact with them in Cape May County.

JP: Do you have any female deputies?

Plousis: Yes. I have 111 deputies that are females. I have a female sergeant, as a matter of fact. And I had a female lieutenant until two years ago, and she retired.

JP: And how long have you had women on your force?

Plousis: The sheriffs have led the way in having females in law enforcement.

JP: You mean in general?

Plousis: General, nationwide. There are more females working for sheriffs' departments than city police or the state police. Traditionally, we employ more women than other agencies. That figure has held true.

JP: Why is that?

Plousis: I think that we've dealt with women more because we have always had female inmates. So the transition of bringing them in, I don't think was so dramatic for county sheriffs as it was for city or state police, who've never had any dealings with women. That number has certainly increased over the last twelve years. But what I'm getting at is that historically, in order to address female inmates, you always had to have female officers. So we were acclimated to them long before the local police or the state police.

JP: Can you tell me what was your most exciting case? Before you tell me that, I'm assuming that you, like Sheriff Froehlich, have mainly administrative tasks?

Plousis: I'm afraid so. Budget and personnel allocation does take a lion's share of our time, yes.

JP: Is there any case that stands out in your mind?

Plousis: Well, there's no question. Probably one of the most, the one that would jump to mind is housing the two terrorists from the World Trade Center building. When you have people of that caliber that blew up the World Trade Center, you have thoughts about their ability to try to make an attack on the jail. So for the two days we had those people here, we took extra precaution and we beefed up our security. But there's no doubt that was a trying time. It would be for any sheriff because of the caliber of these inmates.

JP: Please describe the training for your staff.

Plousis: All of our sheriff's officers go through the exact same training as local police. So they would go to the police academy for eighteen weeks and learn all the police procedures. Then when they get out of the academy, we have one week of training that teaches them how to handle the service of papers, how to do fugitive arrest, how to do prisoner transportations and our specialized services. So roughly it's a nineteen-week training. It is the exact same training that city police get, plus an additional week with specialization in the areas that we do more often.

JP: Are most of them college graduates?

Plousis: We have them mixed. We have some that have associates degrees, some with four years, some with none. That is changing. You're getting a better educated officer year after year.

JP: Are your requiring that or is it just happening?

Plousis: No, not at the moment. It's just happening.

JP: Anything else you can share with me?

Plousis: As you know, the sheriffs celebrated their millennium in 1992, and you know the Magna Carta, you know in all three revisions, the sheriff is the most prominent figure in the Magna Carta. Out of the sixty-three articles, twenty-three state or directly relate to the sheriff.

JP: How many times are sheriffs mentioned?

Plousis: Twenty-three times directly or indirectly because in there, there are some references to lower officials such as bailiffs and wardens that would answer to the sheriff. And then if you'd look in the Magna Carta, it's broken into sixty-three segments.

Edited Telephone Interview: Sheriff Capwell—Wyoming County, New York (Characterized as the Dean of Sheriffs)

JP: Why did Chris McBride characterize you as the Dean of Sheriffs?

Capwell: I think 'cause I'm old as dirt. A friend of mine and I started at the same time, and he just died and so I'm left.

JP: How did you get into law enforcement?

Capwell: Well, I'm not really sure. I guess probably a lot of it had to do with my upbringing as far as the interest and involvement. My parents and their people, we come from a real rural area.

JP: Where was that?

Capwell: Well, it's Wyoming County. It's located midway between Buffalo and Rochester, only south down into the hills. Attica prison is in that county. And the county seat is a small village of about five thousand people, and we lived twelve miles outside the county seat. And my dad was in farm service: feed, farm supplies, grocery store, grain, that sort of thing. I went to Alfred to get a degree in rural engineering, and while I was there, I was interested in the police aspect of it. A wee bit before that I'd been a volunteer fireman. By the time I got my degree, I was more interested in police work. So, I worked in my field for about two years, but then a job opened up here in Wyoming County, and I've been here ever since. It's been forty years, February 23rd.

JP: How long is your term?

Capwell: Four years now. When I first started, there were three-year terms, but then we got the constitution amended a few years ago, and it's a four year term now.

JP: Do you agree with that amendment?

Capwell: Oh, yeah. It's extremely difficult to take over any agency and make any meaningful changes and then see if those changes are worthwhile in two or three years. It's terrible for these assemblymen and senators. It really takes four to six years before you can see what, if any, good things you're doing, or bad things.

JP: Tell me what your duties are and how they have changed or evolved.

Capwell: Well, that would be very difficult. Generally speaking, we're the keeper of the peace and the officer of the courts. That takes various aspects of everything from court security to serving civil papers and enforcing court orders, patrol, investigation of complaints, or arrests for criminal acts. Including all those duties, the sheriff also has the corrections aspect of running the governing jail. And the unwritten part is that we're here twenty-four hours a day, and if nobody else will do it, we have to. That's everything from unlocking locked cars with keys inside or transporting mental patients or anything that nobody else does, we end up doing it.

JP: Are you the primary law, as opposed to in New York City where we have a municipal police force?

Capwell: Yes, you do. In New York City you have one sheriff for all five counties, and they are exclusively civil law enforcement. Here, we're full service law enforcement, and we have concurrent jurisdiction with four village police departments, and then, of course, the state police are criminal law enforcement. But we're the only agency that also does civil law enforcement and correctional law. Numerically speaking, considering the other five agencies, we're doing about 80 percent of the criminal investigations here.

JP: You are considered county law, correct?

Capwell: Yes.

JP: From what I hear you saying is that you are responsible for more anticriminal duties than county sheriffs in New Jersey, for instance.

Capwell: That's probably true. I know that the office of sheriff is different in different areas. In Pennsylvania, I think, the office of sheriff is pretty much limited to civil matters. Other states, they may be just civil and corrections, but the vast majority of the states are full service. If I recall correctly, Alaska and Hawaii do not have sheriffs.

JP: What major changes have occurred during your forty years tenure?

Capwell: Well, I guess the two principle things that I can think of is the complexity of rights and investigations, and jumping through the hoops in different court decisions as to what's admissible and what's not admissible. Together with, and we don't see a whole lot of the ethnic problems, but being able to get along with modern trend thinkings as far as philosophy, law enforcement, and everything else. The other is that you see a dramatic increase of people being unable to take care of themselves. There were four deputy sheriffs. We now have twenty-eight, and our population has not increased enough to say so. In the old days if your neighbor's kid threw a rock through your window, you'd paddle them. If he did it twice, you told his dad. Now if that happens, you call a policeman. So we find that we are handling several thousand complaints a year. That's compared to probably five hundred back when I started.

JP: Is that because the "good neighbor" concept has decreased?

Capwell: I think it is. I don't think neighborliness has reduced as much as the fear of liability, plus the liberal attitudes of expecting government to do everything for you. You see the same thing on highways. When I was first driving, I used to have chains on the tires most of the winter to travel. Now you expect the highway department to have the roads squeaky clean, twenty-four hours a day.

JP: Still on that line of thinking, have you seen any dramatic change between the eighties and the nineties?

Capwell: Not too much. We've always enjoyed a good relationship with people. The country was experiencing antagonism towards the police, we still enjoyed a lot of cooperation. And I think we're very fortunate that way. We try to stay very close to the people. For example, all of our officers are required to have lists and telephone numbers.

JP: I've never heard of that before.

Capwell: Quite right. And we also do everything to adjust schedules and things to allow them to participate in the local civics like church, fire department, things like that. So, we try to stay close to the people, and we think that it's really paid off.

JP: Do they also need to stay, to live in the area?

Capwell: Oh, yes.

JP: What was your election platform?

Capwell: I started in, as I said, '56. And then I spent four years in the service and came right back to this job in 1966. The sheriff died in office and the undersheriff became sheriff, and he appointed me as his undersheriff. So I've been here right along. Through the continual involvement in everything and when that sheriff decided to retire, which was, I guess, a year after the Attica prison riots. We had some very close contact there with people. In fact, that's why he retired. He had a lot of friends inside to take over and so forth. Everything just went in the right direction. I've had some pretty stiff competition in almost every election. I just try to do my job and relate to the people as closely as possible all the time so that election year is really not much different than the rest of the time.

JP: And what are the responsibilities of the undersheriff?

Capwell: He's second in command and the acting sheriff in the sheriff's absence, whether vacations or away or whatever. Beyond that we have different offices. In our case the undersheriff has direct supervision of the criminal investigations division and general supervision over everything else. And, of course, in my absence he's in charge of everything.

JP: Does the sheriff still get involved in all the criminal activities or only in special cases, although the municipal police forces are available?

Capwell: The villages only comprise probably 20 percent of the population and less than 10 percent of the area. So, we're automatically involved in the majority of it to begin with. Secondly, since they're supported by local village tax dollars, they're the primary agency, and they should handle things. And we stand ready to assist them. Some things we assist them, we do all of their dispatching, do all their major criminal investigations, all of their scientific evidence collection, and we also provide additional manpower when they have major public functions and things. The other thing would be, both in the villages and outside, if the complainant is dissatisfied with the service he got with a certain agency. So occasionally they'll call us and say they don't like the way we handled such and such a problem.

JP: The residents actually do that, Sheriff Capwell?

Capwell: Oh, yes. And the same thing is true with the village. If they didn't like the village for some reason, they'll call for either us or the troopers to come in and handle their complaint in the village. They don't seem to understand that we all talk to each other, and all work together.

JP: What's the actual, approximate land mass that you have to control?

Capwell: Six hundred two square miles.

JP: Now, that's very similar to out west where the sheriff's department have miles and miles to patrol.

Capwell: Well, yes and no. I think they're probably much bigger than we are. You've got several counties in this state that are bigger than the state of Rhode Island.

JP: Do you have any female deputies?

Capwell: Right now we have one full time and three part-timers and then we have, I guess, five or six female corrections officers.

JP: Could you describe the training that your deputies are involved with?

Capwell: We mandate 440 hours in formal classroom training. In addition, we, as an entrance requirement, require a two-year degree in a major of police science. And then we do in-service training for the rest of their lives.

JP: All your deputies are college trained?

Capwell: No. As they retire, newcomers will be. Probably a third are college degree holders.

JP: Sir, is that similar around the state?

Capwell: No. We're quite unusual. I think there's only one other county that's requiring a degree, and the state police are requiring a degree.

JP: And what county is that?

Capwell: Tennessee County.

JP: Also, I guess I'm right in assuming that other areas don't have college trained sheriffs?

Capwell: I have no idea. I think they run all the gamut from—I wouldn't be surprised if they might not have a high school diploma. Too, we have attorneys admitted to the bar who are sheriffs.

JP: Tell me, what was your most exciting or noteworthy case?

Capwell: Every day is exciting. That's the best part of this job. I'm always anxious to get here and see what the day holds.

JP: Have you had any really desperate people that you had to capture?

Capwell: Oh, I'm sure I'm involved occasionally, but I'm getting a little old to talk about it. Tell you what I'll do. I wrote a book, and I'll send you a copy of it.

JP: Okay, I'd like that. Does your department also do evictions?

Capwell: Yes. In fact, we had a very messy one last fall. What the status is I don't know.

JP: Messy in what way?

Capwell: We had a person who moved a house trailer in on agricultural property, just sat it there and lived in it. And after I don't know how many years of legal proceedings, they decided to evict them. He got the media involved and the militia and so forth. I had to take armed officers there. He did a lot of talking at this point. I guess the town had decided not to evict him.

JP: Do you also have a constable?

Capwell: Yes. Those are town officers.

JP: When you say town, is that the same as village?

Capwell: No. It's another level in the municipal government. There are townships, and that's what I really meant was a township officer. And then you also have incorporated villages and incorporated cities, both of which are inside townships and counties.

JP: And what does the constable do?

Capwell: The constable is principally an officer of the county court and serves justice court papers. In fact, they're what they call peace officers, as opposed to police officers, which we are.

JP: Your officers are process servers. Is that correct?

Capwell: Yes.

JP: Your staff is county while their authority encompasses certain townships.

Capwell: Right. Normally, county or outside the county or state, where peace officers would be within the township only.

JP: Are the peace officer's qualifications similar to officers?

Capwell: I don't believe there are any qualifications.

JP: Are they elected?

Capwell: They're appointed by the town board.

JP: Is there anything else you can share with me?

Capwell: I can't think of anything offhand. Unless you want to know where the word sheriff came from.

JP: That would be helpful.

Capwell: Depending on who you believe, the word is mentioned in the Bible. Some Bible scholars did some research for me. Their translation of the word sheriff is really similar to an attorney, maybe. The first sheriff appeared about 1066 and has evolved since then. In fact, England just had a millennium, a sheriff's celebration. He was the common law for a long time. And we had sheriffs in this country before we were the United States; they were English sheriffs. In fact, in Albany, New York, we had a sheriff appointed by the king for several years.

JP: There's a special word for sheriff?

Capwell: Well, the theory is that the Anglo-Saxon people gave it an Anglo-Saxon name, and it might have come from various things.

JP: Anyone else in your family in law enforcement?

Capwell: No.

JP: Did your family object to your going into law enforcement?

Capwell: Oh, no. They were very supportive. I think the number two daughter would have liked to enter the profession. But I tried to discourage her, I guess.

JP: Why did you do that, sir? Too dangerous?

Capwell: Well, the rewards today are not like that four years ago for instance. There is less accomplishment. But I don't know. I just didn't want to encourage her.

JP: What field did she select?

Capwell: She got a degree in hotel administration, and then almost starved to death. So now she's an accountant for a Ford agency up in Buffalo.

JP: I'm also looking at bounty hunters. Do you have any involvement with them? Any experience with them?

Capwell: No, only what I've seen on television, and I don't watch anymore.

JP: So you don't deal with them at all. Bounty hunters don't go to your county for bail jumpers?

Capwell: No, never seen them.

JP: Do you have many bailbondspersons there?

Capwell: It's very, very difficult to get a bailbond in this area.

JP: Why is that, sir?

Capwell: Probably because it's very little called for. Plus the system now makes it almost unnecessary. We have a partially state-funded person that wanders around here every day getting people out of jail. They get bail reduced or the person released in somebody's custody. The only time we've seen bailbondsmen was during the Attica riots. We get some from New York or Buffalo to come down here to try to bail somebody out. It's very rare.

JP: Is it also that many people in your area get out on their own recognizance?

Capwell: Well, you see this is another whole philosophy. We have justice courts in each township and each village.

JP: What are their purpose?

Capwell: They are locally elected judges that are very close to the people in the village, and they exercise the judgment. Then, you have a system where their attorney is a public defender and can appeal that judgment in the county court. Many times a person will be held in jail overnight or a weekend until the situation calms down and then they're released in their own custody. Or in some cases where they look like transients, bail might be required. There are very few people that we get that are held for trial any length of time by not making bail.

JP: Would you say that crime has gone up in your area? I know the state has decreased, but. . . .

Capwell: For a long time we were probably going up anywhere from 2 to 10 percent every year, seems like for the last twenty years.

JP: Why was that?

Capwell: Well, one of my feelings would be for lack of punishment, for lack of certainty of punishment. Now they accept things that they wouldn't accept twenty or forty years ago. Due to mobilization and transportation, people from Buffalo, Rochester, get out here, get back. There are more people moving into the county that don't have ties. Therefore, neighbors don't recognize the stranger. They don't feel a responsibility to do something if they see something going down.

JP: What kind of crimes?

Capwell: Oh, everything. Rape, burglaries, assaults, murders. We certainly have a lot fewer numbers than you see in the metropolitan counties, but we have them.

JP: Has it begun to decrease now?

Capwell: The last report showed a very slight decrease.

JP: Would you agree that the decrease had something to do with the age of the population?

Capwell: No, I wouldn't.

JP: And are there primarily middle age or younger people in your county?

Capwell: I guess I don't have the foggiest idea. I don't see any difference. The vast majority of our inmates are younger people. You very rarely see an inmate that's over thirty.

JP: An aging population would certainly decrease crime, but I guess what I hear you saying is that's not the case there.

Capwell: Not that it's very apparent at least. I don't detect any big shift.

JP: Okay. Well, thank you, sir. Again unless there's something that you would like to share with me I would appreciate hearing it.

Capwell: I don't think so.

NINETEENTH-CENTURY COUNTY SHERIFFS

There are people who place the sheriff's origins in ancient Rome. It is mentioned in the Bible's Old Testament, Book of Daniel. Others trace its beginnings prior to the Magna Carta, in England, circa 1215. For sure, it is the oldest law enforcement agency in English common law, dating back over a thousand years. The sheriffs' position in England had been powerful and, until recently, answerable only to the king and serving the wealthy class. Before police, judges, and magistrates, there were sheriffs. They made arrests, raised armies, collected taxes and levies, presided over courts, and handled prisoners. Most important, sheriffs were entrusted with the preservation of domestic tranquillity.

Although the sheriffs in North America are patterned after English tradition, there is a distinct difference between them. An English sheriff receives an appointment, and currently, it is a position that is largely ceremonial.[1] Sheriffs in the American colonies, territories, and later the United States are, by and large, elected. They perform various duties in addition to law enforcement. Subtle differences emerge in other countries the British colonized, including Australia, Canada, and New Zealand. Stated another way, wherever the British formed and dominated a nation's government, the sheriff's office and title were usually established as official peace officers. This shrieval institution, implemented in the southwest in 1846, has survived throughout the years and assisted in bringing progress, through law enforcement, to major areas of the nation, as well as developing the frontier.[2]

To their credit, a few courageous pioneer women played integral roles as peace officers on the nation's expanding western territory. Linda Scott served as acting sheriff in Apache County, Arizona, from 1894 to

1896, filling in for her husband while he was away on business. She kept records and attended to the tax money her husband collected. Presumably, male deputies handled all the criminal activity. The first female deputy was appointed in 1914. Other counties installed deputies who were females, in 1915 and 1918.[3] However, this story is moving too fast. A review of frontier sheriffs in the early 1800s is important and justified. (Sheriffs are depicted as males in this era since, according to my research, women served primarily when the male representative was absent.)

Frontier peace officers in the Arizona and New Mexico territories basically duplicated their eastern colleagues' structures.[4] Staff selections, maintaining jails and prisoners, together with recordkeeping are a few of the official duties for which they were responsible. The county's size, over which the sheriffs had jurisdiction, was massive. Even when Arizona and New Mexico territories were separated, the challenge remained formidable. One sheriff implied that his county was nearly the size of Russia.[5] In addition to such dauntingly huge counties that required policing, sheriffs had equally important daily tasks.

Explains historian Larry Ball, while acknowledging and affirming the law officers' allegiance to those who elected them, "the Sheriff exercised many functions and served many masters. As the county executive officer he answered to the board of supervisors in Arizona and in New Mexico to the commissioners."[6] The sheriff's duties also encompassed serving processes—warrants, subpoenas, and other documents when court was in session. He was the ex-officio tax assessor and collector of taxes and license fees. As peacekeeper, he was empowered to raise the posse comitatus when circumstances became particularly violent.

Having so many official responsibilities, together with managing a private business, left the sheriff scant time for a personal life. Therefore, either his wife worked, gratis, as office clerk or he hired a chief deputy. "A jailer and four or five general (field) deputies rounded out the main office."[7] In the New Mexico territory, sheriffs were permitted a designated number of deputies; not so in Arizona. Sheriffs' qualifications were few. Required were: citizenship, no prison record, and a good reputation. Still, exclusivity and nepotism were the rule. Native Americans were seldom considered for employment even if they wanted the job.

People without property, many of whom having had brushes with the law, were disqualified for deputyships. Essentially, sheriffs hired people like themselves, especially family members and friends. As elucidated above, nepotism was the norm, an accepted practice in both territories. Formal education was not an issue. Concomitantly, official records noted "that southwestern Peaceofficers were seldom illiterate."[8]

Nevertheless, some deputy sheriffs, John Owen in New Mexico for instance, claimed his superior could hardly write his name.

A vital requirement was that sheriffs post two bonds for working as lawman and tax collector. The sheriff had a badge with the office's symbol, originating in England's Middle Ages, "when the Sheriffs . . . were aristocratic knights [and] insisted upon heraldry and pageantry as signs of their status."[9] On the frontier, small businesspeople crafted sheriffs badges in various styles, with title and county. When entrepreneurs were absent, sheriffs used their creativity and designed their own badges. Ball noted that some badges were famous, one having been made of pure gold, and another had a diamond in the center. Prescott, Arizona, officials stipulated that sheriffs present incoming colleagues with the badge. In other words, it was county property. Presumably, the era of lavish badges ended with that regulation.

Also of interest was the condition of public buildings. They were less than appropriate for any official law enforcement purposes, particularly the jails and sheriffs' offices. Major repairs were so desperately needed that, in some cases, sheriffs operated out of their business offices, even their homes. In other instances, repairs were made with private funds. Jails were horrendous if they existed at all. It is known that at one time an unused mine tunnel was converted to a jail. Another time, prisoners were shackled and left outside. In addition, they were kept in the peace officer's house with food expenses absorbed by the sheriff's personal funds. Plumbing for prisoners sometimes consisted of a bucket of water by day and an empty bucket by night.[10]

In terms of remuneration, sheriffs and deputies received pay for serving processes, together with a percentage of each task performed (see Table 4.1). These fees were the result of a notion that sheriffs work harder under a system of piecework. Fees differed between Arizona and New Mexico, from 1846–1887. A case in point: In 1846 executing a death warrant in New Mexico yielded $15.00. By the 1880s, sheriffs of both states earned $50.00 for executing a death warrant. After collecting all the fee vouchers of the sheriff and his deputies, he presented the receipts for reimbursement by his board of supervisors, then paid the deputies and office bills, keeping whatever sum was left.

Deputy Sheriff Wyatt Earp, Cochise County, Arizona, charged that Sheriff Behan took in $40,000 a year, an unlikely occurrence. The average sheriff, like Pat Garrett, earned only about $6,000 a year. Admittedly, there was inherent abuse in this system. Allegedly, peace officers (and deputies) devoted more to process serving than apprehending criminals. Providing a salary was a partial answer to impropriety charges together with punishing sheriffs and deputies for their cavalier approach to jail breaks or criminal apprehension. There were instances when a frontier county or town decreed that the sheriff would

Table 4.1
Kearny Code: Fee System for Sheriffs and Other Lawmen, New Mexico Territory, 1846

Code	Fees
Service of a warrant	$1.00
Levying execution (civil)	$1.00
Summoning jurors	$0.50
Summoning witnesses	$0.50
Attending court (daily)	$1.50
Calling each witness	$0.05
Summoning grand jury	$5.00
Commitment of prisoners to jail	$1.00
Support of prisoner (daily)	$0.25
Executing death warrant	$15.00
Mileage (per mile)	$0.05

Source: Larry Ball, "Frontier Sheriffs at Work," *Journal of Arizona History* 27.3 (1986): 292.

serve out the escapees' sentence. In other cases, a town would add fugitive recovery to the fee system, a form of bounty, despite the possibility of wrongful identification or imprisonment.

Regardless of such hardships, there was no dearth of men seeking the office because it held future political possibilities. Thus, we see the full range and breadth of western sheriffdom. Sheriffs were the de facto benefactors of bounty hunters when they offered rewards. Actually, the peace officers (primarily deputies) turned to bounty hunting at any given time, especially when the rewards were substantial. For example, in 1885 a $500 reward was offered by an Arizona sheriff for the Native American Geronimo, dead or alive—a rather large sum in those days—prompting many people, including law officers, to join the hunt.

Generally speaking, during Arizona's and New Mexico's territorial status, the men who served as sheriffs were adequate for the job, despite being without training and formal education. Working under harsh conditions, frontier sheriffs made the best of primitive facilities, overburdened staff, and a cumbersome fee system. Still, their profession survived and became synonymous with law and order well into the twentieth century. At the spectrum's other end were men who embraced the shrievalty, but disgraced it by their unsavory conduct or colorful nature. These sheriffs or deputies added to the profession's fame, while a few provided notoriety, as will be illustrated in the following true stories.

New Jersey's shrievalty has a long history. In 1739 in Cape May County, "King George II granted a charter to the citizens of the Free Borough and Town of Elizabeth."[11] Town sheriff, town marshal, high constable, and constable were the focus of this document. A June 23, 1980, letter by the Sheriffs Association of New Jersey counsel reviewed "the nature of the Sheriff's office," noting that New Jersey's first constitution, in 1776, had provisions for the annual election of one county sheriff. As Lester Sargent intimated in *A Brief History of the Union County Sheriffs Office*, under English common law the power of the county lay with the sheriff."

In order to keep peace, the sheriff could draft every man to assist in that effort. Such power was termed the posse comitatus and involved preserving the peace, organizing inhabitants of the county or shire for military purposes, managing royal estates, collecting taxes, enforcing the king's commands, taking custody of prisoners, serving writs to institute court proceedings, as well as executing judgments of the court. As is apparent, the southwest sheriff's office was established after the original colonies' institutions; the latter, in turn, adopted English common law.

New York City Sheriffs

New York City's sheriff's office is very old, but with completely different responsibilities than the previously discussed county sheriffs. By March 1655 the office was under Dutch rule, and it was already an entrenched institution: "the schout or Sheriff informs the burgomasters and schepens that some of the company (soldiers) and servants will seek permission to tap beer."[12] However, the sheriff opposed the action because he believed it would lead to debauchery and irregularities. Consequently, the board immediately refused the permit. At times, legal actions were swift. In an earlier February (1655) provisional council the same sheriff, whose title was listed as provisional secretary, discussed his intention of appointing a "Concierge" (high constable, baliff, or city Marshal); the exact date was not stated. He asked "if they have anything against it?" Council made the appointment with the city court's approval.[13]

His commission was signed by the sheriff who doubled as the council's provincial secretary, the exact title was not stated—constablry or city marshal. Duties encompassed "the maintenance of justice and the execution of judgments that were rendered either by the Council or the City court in civil cases." It was duly noted that "Stuyvesant was absent on his journey to Curacao when the appointment was made, but he knew of the proposal on December 17, a week before his departure."[14] Thus, we see the sheriff's role and position are firmly ensconced in this nation's anticrime and peacekeeping history.

It is apparent that sheriffs' roles and positions are firmly ensconced in the annals of our nation's peacekeeping initiatives. Historical records

Table 4.2
Sheriffs' Fees, New York City

Duties	Fees
Summons, Order of Arrests	$1.00
Travel a mile, same for two or more mandates	$0.06
Warrant of Attachment or executing a requisition to replevy	$1.00
Making & filing description of real property or inventory	$0.25
Each copy for each folio	$0.12
Appraisers for each day as Judge allows	$2.00
Advertising pending action on personal property attached	$2.00
Entitled to poundage on the value of the property attached before or after judgment	
Copy of summons, Mandate, complaint Affidavit or other paper served where no fee is prescribed by law	$0.12 (each folio)

Source: Digest of Legal Fees for the State of New York (Rochester, N.Y.: Clinton Moon Publishers, 1890), 27.

show that by the late 1800s their responsibilities had increased. Moreover, politicians institutionalized the remuneration sheriffs received. These fees (see Table 4.2) provided an incentive for them to devote all their time and energy to policing duties rather than engage in personal enterprises.

True Story

Sheriff Shibell assumed his position in Pima County, Arizona Territory, in 1877, working hard for four years bringing law and order to "three thousand residents . . . scattered over twelve thousand acres."[15] Mike Anderson, historian, characterized Shibell as a joiner with membership in the ancient Order of United Workmen and the Society of Arizona Pioneers, and as a family man, father of six children.[16] Shibell was well liked and counted among his friends people across the political spectrum. Although a significant amount of time was spent tracking criminals in his massive county, Shibell's primary efforts encompassed tending bureaucratic duties, including executing court directives, tax assessments and collection, and housing or transporting mentally ill people.

He is distinguished in shrievalty history in three ways. First, he took just one life during his entire twelve-year law enforcement career. Although, interestingly, Shibell killed the suspect in an ambush, he was never criticized by his constituents or opponents. Anderson observes that residents who approved of lynch law would have no qualms about a criminal's well being or rights. Second, Shibell appointed Wyatt S. Earp as a deputy in Tombstone, thus, some would contend, setting the stage for the subsequent gunfight at the O.K. Corral (in actuality, the battle was held elsewhere). In due time, his actions (or nonresponse) in that tragic gunfight would muddy his name and character. Third, he was the major player in a sheriff's election marred by fraud, even though, or perhaps because, it was Pima County's first foray into formal party politics. The election was characterized by the appointments of the infamous Johnny Ringo and Ike Clanton as election officials. Eventually, after a long court battle, election results were declared invalid. Robert H. Paul assumed his rightful position as sheriff, receiving the coveted badge on April 25, 1881, according to the *Arizona Weekly citizen* (275).

Colorful sheriffs were as prevalent in New Mexico as in other states. Sheriff William Brady's exploits are arguably legendary and well known throughout the nation, for instance. A perusal of his tenure is like reading a novel, complete with political intrigue, religious issues, and revolution with the story's roots spread between Irish and English history. Brady, a Roman Catholic and the oldest of seven siblings, was born in Ireland to a tenant farming family in 1829. Indeed, his place of birth was among the original counties in England's plantation system. Protestant landlords kept the Catholic peasants virtually enslaved.

After emancipation and the subsequent potato famine in 1851, Brady left Ireland to live in North America. In due course, following a military stint, Brady became sheriff of Lincoln County. Brady's critics maintain he was Lawrence Murphy's willing tool. The latter held sway as a political and economic czar in New Mexico's wild 1870s. Further, opponents believed that Brady gave Murphy the law's full backing during the Lincoln County war. Two camps of gangs composed of Irishmen and Englishmen fought over issues formed by "land fraud(s), outlaws, crooked politicians, swindlers and dishonest local elected officials."[17]

Author Donald Lavash maintains that "the struggle in Lincoln . . . was a continuation of the conflict between England and Ireland that has plagued the Irish for centuries. Proportedly it became a struggle, . . . that involved, among other things, commerce, [still] within this hostile greedy climate in Lincoln, efforts were being made to advance principles of good government."[18] But embezzlement and murder charges were in the courts for years. Southwest writer Robert Utley observes that the code of the war was founded in whiskey.[19] He provides these thought-provoking observations: "The litany of shootings in Lincoln during the 1870s as set down in newspapers, betrays whiskey almost invariably as an ingredient; and not only drunken riffraff. Time and time again prominent citizens shot it out as well."[20]

Utley found it important to review the various terms and definitions as they related to Lincoln County. Specifically, "Regulations . . . men assembled to regulate or to set right an intolerable situation." Vigilantism, an ancient practice where victims were executed on one pretext or another, "formed in the absence or breakdown of the regular law enforcement and judicial machinery."[21] In Lincoln County "the machinery had not broken down, it had simply been captured by the other side."[22] Of interest, comments Utley, is that vigilantes were comprised of the upper and middle classes in concert against the lower class; that is, the better sort, the business and political elite, sought to control the powerless people who vastly outnumbered them.

Eventually, says Utley, "the man behind the badge practiced a highly personal capricious brand of enforcement,"[23] arresting law breakers when and if they saw fit. Be that as it may, Sheriff Brady, while attempting to carry out the duties of his office was assassinated (April 1878) by killers hired for a $500 reward and involved with Billy the Kid. The latter, in turn, was killed by Sheriff Pat Garrett in July 1881.

Back east, law officers engaged in criminal behavior were less in the showcase genre. In 1889, the sheriff in Jersey City, New Jersey, was given the power to select county grand juries by the state legislature. Ballot box stuffers were nervous because the sheriff could send them to jail. Notwithstanding, they had nothing to fear from Sheriff Davis since he was Hudson County's undisputed political boss and the ballot box stuffer head. Davis would certainly not prosecute those underlings, knowing his mayoral campaign would suffer. The president of the police board was asked whether any arrests were to be made and commented insolently that he had not decided yet. Still, the ballot box stuffers continued worrying about an investigation by Trenton officials although Sheriff Davis was Hudson County's club leader. But, the Hudson County ring was victorious.

Taking into account the foregoing stories, one may have envisioned a frontier sheriff's life fraught with mayhem and death. In many respects, that would be an accurate presumption. Nevertheless, the majority of sheriffs survived the challenges, dying at home. Some attained a modicum of wealth, along with fame and respect, using the position to become important players on the political scene. Sheriffs as we know them may not survive through the twenty-first century because a growing number of critics believe their duties should be privatized, thereby saving taxpayers' money. All the same, dismissing them out of hand would be a gross mistake. A thousand-year history illustrates the office's resilience and strength. Leaving it for dead is foolhardy.

5

CONCLUSION

SUMMARY

This book documented aspects of law enforcement that seldom make headlines. Indeed, bounty hunters, city marshals, and constables try to avoid publicity. Sheriffs and U.S. marshals are the exceptions. The former seeks the spotlight because he/she must campaign for office. The research provided a microscopic view of the consequences of the United States' centuries old economic program. Specifically, these issues involve unequal wealth, insufficient jobs, and the need to control the masses. These issues constitute law enforcement linchpins historically in England and the twentieth-century United States.

When we examine the bounty hunting profession, it is immediately apparent that, basically, men with limited education, vocational training, or livable wage prospects turned their energies to an interesting, well-paid trade that had the least formal requirements and supervision. However, opponents maintain that twenty-first century enforcement does not need the services of bounty hunters (bail enforcement agents). The present-day technology utilized by the large municipal, county, and state police forces render bounty hunters obsolete.

Critics are uncomfortable with an expanding coterie of private surrogate law enforcers whose authority supersedes civil service police. Of particular concern are the increasing number of sometimes fatal mistakes made by these men and women; as their ranks increase, again economic considerations are at the forefront. That is, fewer livable wage positions for those without higher education degrees and a burgeoning prison industry provide continuous recruits to the bounty hunting profession. Whether U.S. taxpayers have the opportunity to determine if civil servants can better accomplish those identical duties is in the hands of researchers and concerned people. Privatization of law enforcement may be less expensive. But is democracy, as we know it, diminished in such a structure?

In the late twentieth century, a closeness among bounty hunters is forming, similar to that of a municipal police force. To wit, the profession currently has an organization that looks out for its interests. This association, akin to a club, was founded by Bob Burton, a talented, experienced, long-time bounty hunter, Marine, and soldier of fortune. He is a dedicated president and a parent figure to the younger members.

The organization is growing in membership and expertise as well as fast becoming a powerful lobbying institution. Those self-proclaimed loners of yesteryear are fading from the scene, realizing the importance of strength in unity. Today's technicians of surrogate law enforcement may or may not recognize that a stagnant, depressed, or turbulent economy increases their remuneration; this situation brings to mind an old saying, to paraphrase: One person's hardship is another person's gain.

The bounty hunters' star is rising; they could conceivably be among the twenty-first century's newest highly paid policing specialists. Stated differently, privatization in law enforcement is a windfall for bounty hunters. Actually, this direction in crime control is not a new development. Frank Donner reminds us, in the book *Protectors of Privilege*, that the privately owned Pinkerton Agency, in the colonial era, was the enforcement entity of choice by the wealthy. Established during the Civil War era, Pinkerton's infiltration and military espionage gained fame. Their early twentieth-century notoriety stemmed from antiunion and strikebreaking activities.

Notice how economic and class issues emerge and coalesce. Characteristically, people having insufficient means secure the best employment possible, despite the fact that they are working against those of similar economic status. Acquiring wealth in the United States, indeed the world, is often accomplished at great cost. Precedents established by Pinkerton's could be harbingers of the future expansion of private informants and undercover police. Attracted by the substantial wages, these fledgling crimefighters and domestic unrest controllers will, by race and gender, be a mixed group. Predictably, under those circumstances the bounty hunting association's membership will also become more diverse.

City marshals, operating in the East's urban areas, share common tasks with county sheriffs and constables. These collection agents have long been examples of privatization. Specifically, government activities are carried out by private sector businesspeople. They are the forerunners of privatizing government functions. City marshals are ancillary enforcement and political sycophants working in tandem with entrepreneurs and city government. They receive substantial remuneration for doing almost whatever is necessary to obtain the payment of outstanding debts. To that end, city marshals must sometimes face dangerous challenges, and they rise to the occasion. Given that their history spans centuries, the city marshals' resilience and power are not surprising.

Performing unpleasant, even inhumane, activities on behalf of influential people, the city marshals' success and accumulation of resources are assured. Class issues are obvious in this paradigm. Once again, residents of modest means labor mightily for those with money and power against those who lack sufficient power or influence.

U.S. marshals differ significantly from the professions discussed in this research. Marshals are essentially generalists. This federal police force created by Congress in 1789, serving at the President's behest, have few specified jurisdictions. In other words, U.S. Marshals can do anything and go anywhere at Congress' and the president's discretion. Basically, U.S. marshals support and staff federal courts in their judicial districts as well as provide local federal representation. The marshals' diverse tasks and responsibilities support the notion of their being law enforcement generalists. They have and continue to respond to interesting assignments. According to author Frederick Calhoun, over the past two hundred years at Congress' and the president's request, duties have included: registering enemy aliens, capturing people who were fugitives from enslavement, sealing American borders against armed expeditions aimed at a foreign country, and exchanging spies with the former Union of Soviet Socialist Republics.

In addition, they can raise a posse. U.S. marshals are unique, and are the sole barrier between civilian government and military rule. Stated plainly, their uniqueness stems from the fact that our democracy is in their hands at all times. For all intents and purposes, they are beholden to the people, despite being answerable to Congress and the president. A case in point: "early on the federal government adopted measures to make its authority more palatable to the American people. Those who enforced federal laws at the local level generally came from that locality. They understood the people, for they were dealing with their friends and neighbors," said Calhoun, chronicler for the U.S. marshals' *The Lawmen: U.S. Marshals and Their Deputies 1789–1989*.

He continued, "unless they were prepared to leave their homes after their commissions expired, the USM [U.S. Marshals] struggled to balance the enforcement of federal laws against the feelings of the local populace. . . . They did not carry out orders blindly. In the months immediately before the opening of the Civil War, marshals throughout the south resigned. . . . Pushed to the limit these Marshals choose loyalty to their communities over obedience to the federal government" (Calhoun, 6). It is doubtful the aforementioned situation would repeat itself in the twenty-first century. As participants in the patronage system, U.S. marshals in the colonial era were less than professional, paying more attention to their political mentors' needs and concerns.

There were numerous abuses inherent in that structure. Some would contend that the prescribed actions in the 1890s are examples of reproachful behavior. As the United States struggled through cataclysmic changes, from a rural to an urban society, from an agricultural base to industry, U.S. marshals were used against workers who organized and challenged corporate power. "Federal judges colluded among themselves, with the United States attorneys and Marshals . . . to suppress strikes" (Calhoun, 207). Officials viewed workers' organizing efforts as an affront or challenge to the nation's system of government, not a dispute with corporations. Accordingly, they used full force against workers in support of business. In many aspects, this was at once an oppressive and telling yet exciting chapter in U.S. history.

Conceivably, that scenario could not be repeated in the twenty-first century. School desegregation catapulted U.S. marshals into the present-day national conscience in the 1960s. Pictures of U.S. marshals escorting African American children past vicious opponents of desegregation were seen around the world. Regardless of personal desegregation views, presidential directives were implemented. Presumably, most U.S. residents watched proudly as U.S. marshals and deputies enforced our nation's law.

Like all institutions, the marshals' reputation has both been tarnished and has glittered. Changes are in place that strengthen and enhance congressional efforts to eliminate patronage. Since 1973, the service has been given full authority to supervise and hire their deputies. That was a big step in the right direction. U.S. marshals are still appointed by the president. The twentieth-century structure provides lawpersons and residents alike with an adherence to law in a democratic atmosphere. We are a nation of laws, rather than men, and not solely "protectors of privilege" (see Donner, *Protectors of Privilege*).

Sheriffs are the trail blazers in terms of democratically discharging legal imperatives. Through an election, a sheriff assumes his or her position with the community's direct permission. Only sheriffs traverse the uncertain electoral paths. Some twenty-first century sheriffs have centered their legal imperatives in the context of developing and promoting community-based institutions. In short, their brand of law enforcement is people friendly.

Witness the numerous neighborhood initiatives designed, implemented, and administered by sheriffs' departments. Critics note that fear of being eliminated is the mother of invention, hence the push to diversify. Despite the sheriffs' actions, opponents blatantly contend that sheriffs and constables are expensive anachronisms and should be abolished. Whether or not those critics' complaints are justified is an issue that should receive a national hearing. It would be truly ironic if this elected office is terminated without input and public scrutiny. Admittedly, continuing this office may or may not be appropriate as the nation enters a new century.

However, all things considered, sheriffs have updated their profession and carved an important, useful niche beyond law enforcement. Granted, the sheriffs' history is checkered with too many unsavory men, past and present, throughout the nation. It is unfortunate that these early patrolmen were compelled to police larger and larger areas, which resulted in less contact with average constituents and more time among the well-connected or criminal elements. Given the nation's extravagant number of policing agents, mostly uncalled for or unwanted by the electorate, the sheriff's position may not warrant the anachronism label.

Numerous issues together with the initial questions have surfaced in this research, among them, surrogate versus public law enforcement agents and the former's entrepreneurial activities. Beginning with city marshals', entrepreneurship under the auspices of a tax supported entity is an oxymoron at best and could be considered unethical. A public discussion of the city marshals' continued existence is imperative. Their activities require a specific control process and watchful public.

This strategy should also be employed for bounty hunters. Although their organization is a crucial first segment of its professionalism birth, its membership is relatively small, leaving hundreds, perhaps thousands, unaffiliated and operating without any control. The organization should not be expected nor permitted to watch and sanction its members.

Bob Burton, president of the Bail Enforcement Agents Association, admits there are thousands of people in the business of bail enforcement, bodyguards, missing persons finders, and so forth that are virtually unsupervised. Explains Burton, these people, using a computer, telephone, and paid contacts in sensitive-information occupations, have access to a tremendous amount of information, which they utilize to carry out their assignments. Their detection abilities are phenomenal. Yet they and their activities remain essentially hidden from view, comments Burton. Bounty hunters, or bail enforcement agents, are a shadowy force, operating on society's fringes.

Under this system, they collaborate with public law enforcement entities. Whether officially employed by private bailbondspersons or unofficially asked to do favors for law persons who are constrained by public mandates, unregulated and undocumented connections continue. These private entrepreneurs operate far outside public scrutiny and insufficient controls. As noted previously, the increase of large sums one can earn as a bounty hunter are telling and devastating indictments of an economic system that often reinforces and promotes criminal behavior while weakening our democratic institutions.

RECOMMENDATIONS

In the United States, most entrepreneurial efforts operate under some basic, specific restraints and guidelines. Public oversight increases when specific products are involved (medical, automobiles, household items, etc.). Yet, bounty hunters or bail enforcement agents have only minimum restrictions even though their business entails stalking and capturing people. The establishment of a professional union or organization that offers training and an ethics code are certainly critical steps forward. However, a thorough review of the statute that empowers bounty hunters is long overdue.

The armed private residents with more power than publicly funded crimefighters are an inappropriate holdover from English law that requires immediate attention, possibly rescinding. A mockery is made of our democracy and the U.S. Constitution when private businesswomen and -men can track and transport people across national and international borders or forcibly enter residences without warrants. Recently, a couple was mistakenly killed by people who claimed (and later denied) to be bounty hunters. This case may galvanize politicians and the electorate to intervene, thus ending unaccountable authority and power in the United States. A national oversight agency, bureau, or commission on bounty hunters needs to be authorized and established immediately. Perhaps there should be a broad discussion concerning the privatization of law enforcement.

New York City marshals are additional examples of contradictory, English-founded, semipublic surrogate policing agents. They earn thousands of dollars confiscating private property and assets. These armed creditor agents should be ensconced with city sheriffs. Having two nearly identical entities are unnecessary, expensive, and potentially dangerous. An evaluation of New York City marshals and sheriffs, complete with an examination and comparison of budgets and earnings, is warranted. In addition to a review of mandates, for instance using computer models to determine the continued existence of the two agencies, is necessary. At minimum, total separation of responsibilities is justified. To wit, New York City sheriffs could handle the city's deadbeat problems, while the New York City marshals could work solely in the private sector, with both under one supervising public entity.

County sheriffs' critics have mounted quite plausible campaigns to eliminate that position, contending that sheriffs are redundant, costly, and superfluous in the 1990s. That thesis is plausible. Nevertheless, the debate and decision on this issue should be inclusive and left to the electorate. The twentieth century is almost history. Examining, restructuring, or eliminating some of the nation's oldest policing institutions may be long overdue. In other public arenas the process has long been underway. The end is in sight for major social programs once thought to be practically sacred. Witness the attacks leveled against social security, public housing, and medical assistance. The federal commissions' and agencies' legal aid are struggling to remain intact. Public assistance for women and children has virtually ended.

The mantle of sacredness should not be applied to law enforcement agencies because some think that reform is unnecessary. Constant fear of domestic disturbances, preparation, and prevention have no place in a democracy unless the government has turned its back on maintaining a high quality of life for the majority of its people. Some would argue that far too many people in the United States are officially armed and involved in policing as well as corrections. Efforts to obtain precise numbers of licensed armed public personnel were to no avail. This information is not centrally collected, counted, or exchanged, at least as far as could be determined in this research. One bureaucrat confided that the exact numbers of armed civil servants are unknown.

The following partial list is instructive, in that these public agencies have their own enforcement entities. They are additions to municipal police, state police, and the officers discussed in this text.

- *Federal*: Internal Revenue Service; Alcohol, Tobacco, and Firearms; Bureau of Indian Affairs; Central Intelligence Agency; Federal Bureau of Investigation; National Security Council; Secret Service; White House Police; Justice Department; Treasury; Attorney General; Park Rangers; Capitol Police; Hospitals

- *States*: Governor's Office; State House; State Police; Sheriffs; State Office Buildings; Park Rangers; Attorney General; State Welfare Department; Hospitals

- *City*: Undercover Police; Social Services; Hospitals, Armed body guards and chauffeurs for all high ranking political figures

The preceding is included as a wake-up call, advising that far too many officials are armed. At minimum, a precise count should be undertaken and made readily available to the public. Surrogate law agents, along with thousands of armed bureaucrats, are the nightmare colonial and frontier immigrants were most concerned about. And rightly so, because it is now a modern day problem. We forgot to heed history's lessons. Fortunately, we do have the opportunity to reform and save the future.

NOTES

CHAPTER 1: BOUNTY HUNTERS

1. Bob Burton, "An Interview and Book Review Bounty Hunter," *Law and Order: An Independent Magazine for the Police Professional* 32.10 (1984): 130.

2. Ibid.

3. Bob Burton, personal interview, February 1996.

4. "The Jaffe Case and the Use of International Kidnapping as an Alternative to Extradition," *Georgia Journal of International and Comparative Law* 14 (1984): 357.

5. Anonymous (names and place changed at interviewee's request), personal interview, August 1996.

6. *Johnson v. Buie*, 312 F. Supp. 1349.

7. Marie Powers, "Private Extradition Companies: A Benefit to the State at the Expense of the Individual?" *San Diego Law Review* 28 (1991): 203.

8. *Taylor v. Taintor*, 16 Wall 366 (1873).

9. Ibid.

10. Brian Reaves, "Pretrial Release of Felony Defenders, 1990," *U.S. Department of Justice, Office of Justice Programs, Bureau of Justice Statistics Bulletin* (1992): 10–11.

11. Ibid.

12. Ibid.

13. Bob Burton, *Bounty Hunter* (Boulder, Colo.: Paladin Press, 1984), 78.

14. Ibid., 97.

15. Ibid., 99.

16. Ibid.

17. New York City Police Department, Office of the Deputy Commissioner–Legal Matters, *Legal Bureau Bulletin* (New York: 1991), 21.

18. Ibid.

19. *Taylor v. Taintor*, 16 Wall 366 (1873).

20. *Bail Reform Act of 1984*, 18 USC S 3142 (b)(c)(1)(A).

21. Reaves, "Pretrial Release," 11.

22. Robert Kenny, "Dealing with Tax Bounty Hunters," *New Jersey Law Journal* (1995): 11.

23. Ibid.

24. Peter Moses, "Little Lynette Bounty Hunter," *New York Post*, 9 April 1989, 3.

25. Richard Patterson, *Historical Atlas of the Outlaw West* (Boulder, Colo.: Johnson Books, 1985), 13.

26. Use of the pronoun "he" is employed throughout this chapter because the research revealed no female bounty hunters in this time period.

27. Stuart Traub, "Rewards, Bounty Hunting and Criminal Justice in the West: 1865–1900" *The Western Historical Quarterly* 19.3 (1988): 299.

28. Ibid., 297.

29. Robert Utley, *High Noon in Lincoln: Violence on the Western Frontier* (Albuquerque: University of New Mexico Press, 1987), 172.

30. Traub, "Rewards," 288.

31. This is quoted from an unsigned, uncited article on frontier life housed in the Center for Southwest Research files at the University of New Mexico at Albuquerque.

32. Traub, "Rewards," 298.

33. Ibid., 300.

34. Ibid., 299.

35. Marc Simmons, "When Scalping was a Business," *When Six Guns Ruled: Outlaw Tales of the Southwest* (Santa Fe, N.M.: Ancient City Press, 1990), 81–85.

36. Ibid.

37. *The Eagle* (Brooklyn) (1865): 148–49.

38. Traub, "Rewards," 293.

39. Marian Gleason McDougall, *Fugitive Slaves, 1619–1865* (Boston: Ginn and Company, 1891), 48.

40. Ibid.

41. Ibid.

42. *Anonymous Observer: Boston Slave Riot and the Trial of Anthony Burns* (Northbrook, Mass.: Metro Books, 1972), 53.

43. Ibid., 55.

44. Ibid., 60.

45. Ibid.

CHAPTER 2: CITY MARSHALS AND CITY SHERIFFS

1. "Constable Pucks a Pistol [and] Pride as Tops in Her Field," *Daily Sun* (Flagstaff), 2 Jan. 1989: 6.

2. Ibid.

3. New York City Civil Court Act, Art. 16, sec. 1601 no. 3 *Marshals Loose Leaf Law Publications* 3 (1983): 60.

4. Ibid., 61.

5. New York City, Department of Investigation, *Marshals Handbook* (New York: 1986), i.

6. The City of New York, *New York City Budget Review and Comparative Study* (New York: 1978), 50, 51.

7. Ibid.

8. Ibid., 56.

9. "Local Law 440-A," *The Chief Leader*, 20 July 1990, 8.

10. Ken Murray, "He Snaps at Sheriff," *New York Daily News*, 19 May 1992, 3.

11. Frank Prassel, *The Western Peace Officer: A Legacy of Law and Order* (Norman: University of Oklahoma Press, 1972), 49.

12. John Milton Scanland, *Life of Pat F. Garrett Taming of the Border Outlaw: A History of the Gunmen and Outlaws and a Life Story of the Greatest Sheriff of the Old South West* (El Paso, Tex.: El Paso South Western Print Company, 1952), 1–3.

13. Marc Simmons, "The Outlaw Was a Lawman: Milt Yarberry of Albuquerque, Early 1880s," *When Six Guns Ruled: Outlaw Tales of the Southwest* (Santa Fe, N.M.: Ancient City Press, 1990), 56–60.

14. Ibid.

15. Ibid., 60.

16. Ibid.

17. Evans Coleman, "Nesters, Rustlers and Outlaws," *Journal of Arizona History* 14.3 (1973): 179.

18. Richard Patterson, *Historical Atlas of the Outlaw West* (Boulder, Colo.: Johnson Books, 1985), 5.

19. Ibid.

20. I. N. Phelps Stokes, and Robert H. Dodd, *The Iconography of Manhattan Island, 1498–1909* (New York: Arno Press, 1928), 272.

21. Ibid.

22. Ibid.

CHAPTER 3: U.S. MARSHALS

1. U.S. Marshals Service, *Asset Seizure and Forfeiture Fact Sheet, No. 22* (1993).

2. U.S. Marshals Service, U.S. Department of Justice, *Marshals Monitor* 2.3 (1993): 5.

3. U.S. Marshals Service, U.S. Department of Justice, *The Pentacle Bicentennial Edition*, 9.2, updated and reprinted (May 1991): 19. The magazine *The Pentacle* means a five-pointed star-shaped figure. It was formerly used as a mystic symbol and was created with magical powers. In the 1600s, it was believed that a pentacle worn around a soldier's neck would make him invincible to bullets.

4. U.S. Marshals Service, *Prisoner Transportation Fact Sheet, No. 26*, 15 February 1993.

5. Ibid.

6. Ibid., 25.

7. U.S. Marshals Service, *Pentacle*, 15.

8. Frank Prassel, *The Western Peace Officer: A Legacy of Law and Order* (Norman: University of Oklahoma Press, 1972), 229.

9. Ibid., 230.

10. Ibid.

11. Larry Ball, *The United States Marshals of New Mexico and Arizona Territories, 1846–1912* (Albuquerque: University of New Mexico Press, 1978), 240.

12. Ibid.

13. James Long, "Bob Paul, Shotgun Marshal," *Real West* 8.41 (1965): 22.

14. Ibid., 43.

CHAPTER 4: COUNTY SHERIFFS

1. Bud Meeks, "The Sheriff's Millennium: Maintaining Our Proud History," *Sheriff* (Alexandria, Va.) (May–June 1992): 6.

2. Larry Ball, *Desert Lawmen: The High Sheriffs of New Mexico and Arizona 1846–1912* (Albuquerque: The University of New Mexico Press, 1992), 2.

3. Lori Davisson, "Women in Arizona Law Enforcement, 1892–1982," Unpubl. rpt. (Phoenix: Arizona Historical Society, Tucson), 4.

4. Larry Ball, "Frontier Sheriffs at Work," *Journal of Arizona History* 27.3 (1986): 283.

5. Ibid., 284

6. Ibid.

7. Ibid., 285.

8. Ibid., 286.

9. Ibid.

10. Ibid., 291.

11. Lester Sargent, *A Brief History of the Union County Sheriff's Office, April 1857* (Elizabeth, N.J.: Union, County Sheriff's Office, 1993).

12. Stokes and Dodd, *Iconography of Manhattan Island*, 155.

13. Ibid.

14. Ibid.

15. Mike Anderson, "Posses and Politics in Pima County: The Administration of Sheriff Charlie Shibell," *Journal of Arizona History* 27.3 (1986): 253.

16. Ibid.

17. Donald Lavash, *Sheriff William Brady, Tragic Hero of the Lincoln County War* (Santa Fe, N.M.: Sunstone Press, 1986), 12.

18. Ibid.

19. Robert Utley, *High Noon in Lincoln: Violence on the Western Frontier* (Albuquerque: University of New Mexico Press, 1987), 20. Utley also tells us that violence was due to scarce law enforcement and unruly Texas cowboys, and that violence was "through the Texas cowboys to the Texas feud country where it flourished with special virulence. And it had more lethal consequences than at any time in [North American] history, because of the casual attitude toward death and destruction spawned by the civil war and reconstruction."

20. Ibid., 21.
21. Ibid., 57.
22. Ibid., 58.
23. Ibid., 172.

REFERENCES

Abramson, Leslie W. "Extradition in America of Uniform Acts and Governmental Discretion." *Baylor Law Review* 33 (1981): 793–841.

Allen, Otis. *The Duties and Liabilities of Sheriffs in Their Various Relations to the Public and to Individuals. As Governed by the Principles of Common Law and Regulated by the Statutes of New York.* New York: Gould, Banks and Company, 1845.

Anderson, Mike. "Posses and Politics in Pima County: The Administration of Sheriff Charlie Shibell." *Journal of Arizona History* 27.3 (1986): 253–82.

Anonymous Observer: Boston Slave Riot and the Trial of Anthony Burns. Northbrook, Mass.: Metro Books, 1972.

Arce, Rose Marie. "Through a Latin Lens." *New York Newsday*, 28 December 1992, 36.

Arizona Weekly Citizen, 1 May 1881, 275.

Bail Reform Act of 1984, 2nd edition #3, 18 USC S 3142 (b)(c)(1)(A).

Ball, Larry "Commodore Perry Owens, The Man Behind the Legend." *Journal of Arizona History* 33.1 (1992): 27–56.

———. *Desert Lawmen: The High Sheriffs of New Mexico and Arizona, Territories 1846–1912.* Albuquerque: University of New Mexico Press, 1992.

———. "Frontier Sheriffs at Work." *Journal of Arizona History* 27.3 (1986): 283–96.

———. "The Frontier Sheriff's Role in Law and Order." *Western Legal History* 4.1 (1991): 13–25.

———. "Pioneer Lawmen: Crawley P. Drake and Law Enforcement on the South Western Frontier." *Journal of Arizona History* 143.3 (1973): 243–56.

———. "This High-Handed Outrage, Marshal William Kidder Meade in a Mexican Jail." *Journal of Arizona History* 17 (1976).

———. *The United States Marshals of New Mexico and Arizona Territories, 1846–1912*. Albuquerque: University of New Mexico Press, 1978.

Barney, James. "Jim Kenny Ex-Marshal of Phoenix." *The Sheriff* (1945): 53–57.

Barnoff, Sheldon I. "Tax Bounty Hunters; Would They Be Worse Than the Service." *The Journal of Taxation* (1983): 319–22.

Bartholomew, Edward. *Wyatt Earp 1879–1882: The Man and the Myth*. Toyahvale, Tex.: Frontier Book Company, 1964.

Bassiouni, M. Cherif. "Extradition Reform Legislation in the United States 1981–1983." *Akron Law Review* 17 (1984): 495–574.

"Bounty Hunter's Delight." *National Crime Reporter*, May 1978, 1.

"Bounty Hunters: Unusual Service That Tracks Down Bail Jumpers." *Security Letter* 13.2 (1983): 3–4.

Boyle, Stephen. "Transportation of Non-Federal Prisoners." *The Police Chief* 14 (1986): 10.

Burton, Bob. *Bail Enforcer, The Advanced Bounty Hunter*. Boulder, Colo.: Paladin Press, 1990.

———. *Bounty Hunter*. Boulder, Colo.: Paladin Press, 1984.

———. "An Interview and Book Review Bounty Hunter." *Law and Order: An Independent Magazine for the Police Professional* 32.10 (1984): 130.

Calhoun S. Frederick. *The Lawmen: U.S. Marshals and Their Deputies 1789–1989*. Washington, D.C.: Smithsonian Institution Press, 1990.

Campbell, Stanley. *The Slave Catchers: Enforcement of the Fugitive Slave Law 1850–1860*. Chapel Hill: University of North Carolina Press, 1970.

"Canada Sentences Two for Seizing Business Man." *Los Angeles Times*, 11 June 1986, 19.

Capwell, Allen. *The Sheriff of Wyoming County: 150 Years of Protection and Service*. Fillmore, N.Y.: Big Tree Graphics, 1992.

Cheesman, Herrick. *White Servitude in Pennsylvania: Indentured and Redemption. Labor in Colony and Common Wealth*. New York: Negro University Press; 1969.

Cleaveland, Norman, and George Fitzpatrick. "The Morley's—Young Upstarts on the Southwest Frontier." *New Mexico Historical Society* 49 (1974): 258–60.

Coleman, Evans. "Nesters, Rustlers and Outlaws." *Journal of Arizona History* 14.3 (1973): 179.

"*Commonwealth v. Brickett*." *Reports of Cases Argued and Determined in the Supreme Court of Mass.*, March 3, 1829, p. 142.

"Constable Packs a Pistol [and] Pride as Tops in Her Field." *Daily Sun* (Flagstaff), 2 January 1989, 6.

Cousar, Robert, ed. *Digest of the Laws and Decisions Relating to the Appointment Salary and Compensation of the Officials of the US Courts With the*

Instruction of the Attorney General to US District Attorneys, Clerks and Marshals. Washington, D.C.: Government Printing Office, 1895.

"Criminals Pay for Own Capture." *Law and Order: An Independent Magazine for the Police Professional* 40.1 (1992): 4.

Crocker, John. *The Duties of Sheriffs, Coroners and Constables With Practical Forms*. New York: Banks and Brothers, 1890.

Cummings, Homer, and Carl McFarland. *Federal Justice: Chapters in the History of Justice and the Federal Executive*. New York: Macmillan, 1937.

Dance, Darly Cumber. *Long Gone: The Mecklenburg Six and the Theme of Escape in Black Folklore*. Knoxville: University of Tennessee Press, 1987.

Davisson, Lori. "Women in Arizona Law Enforcement, 1892–1982." Unpubl. rpt. Phoenix: Arizona Historical Society, Tucson, 4.

Delfiner, Rita. "Sheriff Will Take Credit Where It's Due: Towed Cars Can Be Ransomed With Plastic Starting June 30." *New York Post*, 13 February 1993, 23.

Diamond, John. "Kidnapping: A Modern Definition." *American Journal of Criminal Law* 13 (1985): 1–36.

Digest of Legal Fees for the State of New York. Rochester, N.Y.: Clinton Moon Publishers, 1890.

Dinkins, David N. *New York City Press Release—Office of the Mayor*, 12 July 1990.

Donner, Frank. *Protectors of Privilege: Red Squads and Police Repression in Urban America*. Berkeley: University of California Press, 1990.

The Eagle (Brooklyn) (1865): 148–49.

Eherts, Walter. "Terror in Taos." *Real West Annual* (Spring 1983): 35.

Eppinga, Jane. "Apache County: Sheriffs Dealt With the Lawful and the Awful." *The Arizona Sheriff* 11.1 (Spring 1992): 12–28.

———. "A Century of Law Enforcement in Maricopa County." *The Arizona Sheriff* 12.2 (Summer 1993): 10–17.

———. Cochise County: Law and Order Did Not Come Easy." *The Arizona Sheriff* 11.3 (Autumn 1992): 12–23.

"Extradition Reforms: The Role of the Judiciary in Protecting the Rights of a Requested Individual." *Boston College International and Comparative Law Review* 9 (1986): 293–322.

Foote, Caleb, ed. *Studies on Bail*. Philadelphia: University of Pennsylvania Law School, 1966.

"For US Bounty Hunters, National Borders Are Little or No Restraint." *Washington Post*, 15 May 1987, 23.

"Fugitives From Justice: Nationwide Manhunt." *Crime Control Digest* 44 (1991): 7.

Geddes, Elaine. "The Private Investigator and the Right to Privacy." *Alberta Law Review* 27 (1989): 256–301.

Gettinger, Stephen. "The Shadowy World of Ralph Thorson." *Police Magazine* 3.3 (1980): 51–56.

Giles, Frances. "Ex-Niagara Sheriff Admits to Stealing Food." *New York Times*, 4 September 1993, 84.

Glennon, Michael J. "State-Sponsored Abduction: A Comment on United States

v. Alverez-Machain [112S. CT 2188 (1992)]." *American Journal of Internal Law* 86 (1992): 746–56.

Goldstein, Tom. "Dropping Of Sheriff's Jury Urged." *New York Times*, 12 December 1976, 78.

"Greater Cleveland: A Bulletin on Public Business." *The Citizens League* (Cleveland), 11 November 1943, 1.

Guide to the Municipal Government of the City of New York. New York: Meilen Press, 1973.

Gullion, Steve. "Sheriffs." *New Law Journal* 142 (1992): 1156.

Hallborg, Robert B. "Principles of Liberty and the Right to Privacy." *Law and Philosophy* 5 (1986): 175–218.

Hayes, Jesse G. *Turbulence in the Arizona Territory*. Tempe: University of Arizona Press, 1968.

Hendrickson, Paul. "Tails They Win Meet Two Very Persistent Guys, A Story of Sleuths and Consequences." *Washington Post*, 26 September 1993, 12.

Hoffman, John. "The Original Resident Police." *Law and Order* 39.9 (1991): 126–127.

Hogan, William. "The Territorial Sheriff in Arizona, 1864–1870." *Journal of Arizona History* 27.4 (1986): 439–50.

Honaker, Marshall. "A Challenge Toward Professionalism." *The Sheriff* 43.4 (1991): 7.

"An Indigent Accused Does Not Have a Constitutional Right to Appointed Counsel at Extradition Hearings: An Analytical Approach." *University of Baltimore Law Review* 13 (1983): 74–91.

"In Re: Henry Siebert." *Reports of Cases Argued and Determined in the Supreme Court of the State of Kansas*, November 11, 1899, *Kansas City Reports*, vol. 61, pp 112–16.

"Interstate Rendition Violations and Section 1983: Locating the Federal Rights of Fugitives." *Fordham Law Review* 50 (1982): 1268–91.

Ito, Timothy M. "Taking the Law into Their Own Hands: Bail Jumpers Keep Bounty Hunters in Business." *U.S. News & World Report*, 21 August 1995, 54.

"The Jaffe Case and the Use of International Kidnapping as an Alternative to Extradition." *Georgia Journal of International and Comparative Law* 14 (1984): 357.

Johnson v. Buie, 312 F. Supp. 1349, 1350, 1351 W.D. MO 1970.

Kelly, Jack. "The Man Behind the Disguise."*USA Today*, 30 August 1993, 64.

Kenny, Robert. "Dealing with Tax Bounty Hunters." *New Jersey Law Journal* (1995): 11.

Khan, A. M. "Double Criminality in Extradition." *The Solicitors' Journal* 129 (1985): 257–59.

Kovaleski, Serge F. "More for This Town's Sheriff?" *New York Daily News*, 21 December 1992, 3.

———. "Move Over, Mayor . . . Mils Are for Marshals." *New York Daily News*, 21 December 1992, 3.

Labaton, Stephen. "New Bounty Hunters Can Make Out Like Bandits." *New York Times*, 17 October 1993, E44.

Lavash, Donald. *Sheriff William Brady, Tragic Hero of the Lincoln County War*. Santa Fe, N.M.: Sunstone Press, 1986.

"Local Law 440-A." *The Chief Leader*, 20 July 1990, 1–8.

Long, James. "Bob Paul, Shotgun Marshal." *Real West* 8.41 (1965): 12–43.

McComb, Henry. *National Municipal Gazetteer* (1893).

McCormick, Robert. "Pima County's First Black Deputy Sheriff, Frank C. Johnson Dead at 82." *Citizen*, 21 August 1989, 3.

McDougall, Marian Gleason. *Fugitive Slaves, 1619–1865*. Boston: Ginn and Company, 1891.

Meeks, Bud. "Executive Director Report: Is Jail a Sheriff's Responsibility?" *Sheriff* 43.1 (1991): 8.

———. "The Sheriff's Millennium: Maintaining Our Proud History." *Sheriff* (Alexandria, Va.) (May–June 1992): 6.

Miller, Rick. *Bounty Hunter*. College Station, Tex.: The Early West Creative Publishing, 1988.

Miller, Wilbur. *Revenuers & Moonshiners: Enforcing Federal Liquor Law in the Mountain South, 1865–1990*. Chapel Hill: University of North Carolina Press, 1991.

Moscow, Warren. *The Chief Leader*, 17 Aug. 1990: 4.

Moses, Peter. "Little Lynette Bounty Hunter." *New York Post*, 9 Apr. 1989: 3–4.

Mullin, Robert. "Here Lies John Kinney." *Journal of Arizona History* 14.3 (1973): 223–42.

Murray, Ken. "He Snaps at Sheriff." *New York Daily News*, 19 May 1992: 3.

Mydans, Beth. "Taking No Prisoners, in Manner of Speaking: A Sheriff Gets Tough and Headlines (Joseph M. Arpaid in Maricopa County, Arizona)." *New York Times*, 4 March 1995, 5.

National Police Chiefs and Sheriffs Information Bureau. *National Directory of Law Enforcement Administration Correctional Institutions and Related Government Agencies*. Milwaukee, 1982.

New York City Civil Court Act. Art. 16, sec. 1601, *Marshals, Loose Leaf Law Publications* 3 (1983): 60–61.

New York City Department of Investigation. *Marshals Handbook*. New York: New York, 1986.

New York City Legislative Office of Budget Review. *New York City Sheriffs, New York City Marshals: A Comparative Study*. New York: City of New York, 1978.

New York City Police Department. Office of the Deputy Commissioner–Legal Matters. *Legal Bureau Bulletin*. New York: 1991.

New York Newsday, 15 April 1992, 93.

New York Post, 9 April 1989, 3.

New York State. "Memorandum of the Civil Service Department Counsel." *McKinney Session Laws of New York*. St. Paul, Minn.: West Publishing Co., 1993.

New York Times, 1 June 1996, 12.

Nieves, Evelyn. "Eleven Bronx Stores Raided As Sheriff Continues Effort to Collect Fines." *New York Times*, 29 November 1990, B2.

"Office of the Sheriff: A 300 Year History of Service to the Citizens of Cape May County." *Annual Report*. Cape May Court House, N.J., 1992.

Patterson, Richard. *Historical Atlas of the Outlaw West*. Boulder, Colo.: Johnson Books, 1985.

Pennsylvania Gazette, 28 January 1728.

Poole, Eric, and Mark Pogrebin. "Deputy Sheriffs As Jail Guards." *Criminal Justice and Behavior* 15 (1988): 190–209.

Powers, Marie. "Private Extradition Companies: A Benefit to the State at the Expense of the Individual?" *San Diego Law Review* 28 (1991): 203.

Prassel, Frank. *The Western Peace Officer: A Legacy of Law and Order.* Norman: University of Oklahoma Press, 1972.

Purdum, Todd S. "A Million-Dollar Question: Who Rescued the Sheriff? New Jersey's Budget Receives $1 Million to Rehire Camden County Sheriff's Officers." *New York Times*, 26 June 1994, 14.

Reaves, Brian. "Pretrial Release of Felony Defenders, 1990." *U.S. Department of Justice, Office of Justice Programs, Bureau of Justice Statistics Bulletin* (1992): 10–11.

Rutherford, Jane. "Beyond Individual Privacy: A New Theory of Family Rights." *University of Florida Law Review* 39 (1987): 627–52.

Sacks, Benjamin. *Arizona's Angry Man: United States Marshal, Milton B. Duffield.* Tempe: Arizona Historical Foundation, 1970.

Safir, Howard. "United States Marshals Service, Fugitive Investigative Strike Teams (FIST)." *The Police Chief* 50.8 (1983): 34–37.

Sargent, Lester. *A Brief History of the Union County Sheriff's Office, April 1857.* Elizabeth, N.J.: Union County's Sheriff's Office, 1993.

Sattler, Ted. "The High Sheriff in England Today: The Invisible Man?" *Sheriff Magazine*, May–June 1992.

Scanland, John Milton. *Life of Pat F. Garrett Taming of the Border Outlaw: A History of the Gunmen and Outlaws and a Life Story of the Greatest Sheriff of the Old South West.* El Paso, Tex.: El Paso South Western Print Company, 1952: 1–3.

"Search by Private Persons: State v. Long [700 P.2d 153 (Wash)]." *Montana Law Review* 47 (1986): 189–206.

Sexton, Joe. "For a Few Dollars More, Bounty Hunters Track Down Fugitive Criminal Aliens." *New York Times*, 12 January 1995, A20.

———. "Hunting Fistfuls of Bounty Dollars An Unusual Freelance Career: Capturing Convicted Aliens." *New York Times*, 12 January 1995, A88.

The Sheriff, May–June 1994: 25.

Sheriff, The Empire State 10 (1995): 2–3.

"Sheriff's Success Breeds Contempt of Rival." *New York Times*, 27 Mar. 1992: A16.

Simmons, Marc. "The Outlaw Was a Lawman." Milt Yarberry of Albuquerque, Early 1880s." *When Six Guns Ruled: Outlaw Tales of the Southwest.* Santa Fe, N.M.: Ancient City Press, 1990.

———. *"When Scalping was a Business." When Six Guns Ruled: Outlaw Tales of the Southwest.* Santa Fe, N.M.: Ancient City Press, 1990.

Somkin, Fred. "The Strange Career of Fugitivity in the History of Interstate Extradition." *Utah Law Review* 3 (Summer 1984): 511–31.

South Carolina Gazette, 2 July 1763. Cited in *Biographical Directory of the South Carolina House of Representatives.* Eds. Walter B. Edgar and N. Louise Baily. Columbia: University of South Carolina Press, 1977: 720–28.

The Star, 15 December 1983, 12.

Stokes, I. N. Phelps and Robert H. Dodd. *The Iconography of Manhattan Island, 1498–1909*. New York: Arno Press, 1928.

Sullivan, Joseph F. "Sheriff Scolded for Attempts to Influence Verdict in Officer's Shooting Trial. (Sheriff Jack Terhund, Bergen County, New Jersey)." *New York Times*, 14 October 1992, A15.

Summer, Martha Hayes. *Vanished Arizona, Recollections of My Army Life*. Philadelphia: J. B. Lippincott Company, 1908.

"Sunrise Surprise." *Law Enforcement News* 17. 347 (1991): 85.

"Symposium: Security of the Person and Security of the State Human Rights and Claims of National Security." *Yale Journal of World Public Order* (1984).

Taylor v. Taintor, 16 Wall 366, 372 (1873).

"Transborder Abductions by American Bounty Hunters—the Jaffe Case and a New Understanding Between the United States and Canada." *Georgia Journal of International and Comparative Law* 20 (1990): 489–504.

Traub, Stuart. "Rewards, Bounty Hunting and Criminal Justice in the West: 1865–1990." *The Western Historical Quarterly* 19.3 (1988): 299.

Twomey, John, and Susan Laniewksi. "The United States Marshals Service Role in the Attorney General's War on Violent Crime." *Journal of Criminal Law and Criminology* 73 (1982): 1012–21.

United States Bureau of Census. *Statistical Abstracts of the United States*. 113th ed. Washington, D.C.: 1993.

United States Constitution, Article IV.

United States Department of Commerce, Economics and Statistics Administration. *Labor Force, Population, Public Aid, Labor Force, Employment and Earnings. Characteristics of the Civilian Labor Force*. Washington, D.C.: 1993.

United States Congress. House of Representatives Annals of Congress. *Compensation of US Marshals, Message from the President, Transmitting Letter from the Attorney General*. 46th Cong., 2d sess. Washington, D.C.: 1880. Executive Documents 21.

United States Marshals Service. *Asset Seizure and Forfeiture Fact Sheet, No. 22* (1993).

———. *Prisoner Transportation Fact Sheet, No. 26*, 15 February 1993.

———. United States Department of Justice. *Marshals Monitor* 2.3 (1993): 5.

———. United States Department of Justice. *The Pentacle Bicentennial Edition* 9.2 (1991): 15–25.

"United Statutes At-Large, 1789, 1842, 1853." *American Historical Review* (1899–1900).

Utley, Robert. *High Noon in Lincoln: Violence on the Western Frontier*. Albuquerque: University of New Mexico Press, 1987.

Walker, Henry. "Retire Peaceably to Your Homes: Arizona Faces Martial Law." *Journal of Arizona History* (1989): 1–18.

Weinberg, John L. *Federal Bail and Detention Handbook*. New York: Practicing Law Institute, 1988.

Wilson, Carol. *Freedom at Risk, The Kidnapping of Free Blacks in America.* Louisville: University of Kentucky Press, 1994.

Wright, Bruce. *Black Robes, White Justice: Why Our Legal System Doesn't Work for Blacks.* Secaucus, N.J.: Carol Publishing Group, 1987.

INDEX

JACQUELINE POPE is an Associate Professor of Political Science, The Richard Stockton College of New Jersey. She is the author of *Biting the Hand That Feeds Them* (Praeger, 1989).